ALLEN CARR

Allen Carr was a chain-smoker for over 30 years. In 1983, after countless failed attempts to quit, he went from 100 cigarettes a day to zero without suffering withdrawal pangs, without using willpower and without putting on weight. He realised that he had discovered what the world had been waiting for – the Easy Way to Stop Smoking, and embarked on a mission to help cure the world's smokers.

As a result of the phenomenal success of his method, he gained an international reputation as the world's leading expert on stopping smoking and his network of clinics now spans the globe. His first book, *Allen Carr's Easy Way to Stop Smoking*, has sold over 12 million copies, remains an international bestseller and has been published in over forty different languages. Hundreds of thousands of smokers have successfully quit at Allen Carr's Easyway Clinics where, with a success rate of over 90%, he guarantees you'll find it easy to stop or your money back.

Allen Carr's Easyway method has been successfully applied to a host of issues including weight control, alcohol and other addictions and fears. A list of Allen Carr clinics appears at the back of this book. Should you require any assistance or if you have any questions, please do not hesitate to contact your nearest clinic.

For more information about Allen Carr's Easyway, please visit **www.allencarr.com**

ALLEN CARR

GET OUT OF DEBT NOW

THE EASY WAY

ARCTURUS

To Tim Glynne-Jones and Nigel Matheson for their invaluable assistance

ARCTURUS

This edition published in 2013 by Arcturus Publishing Limited
26/27 Bickels Yard, 151–153 Bermondsey Street,
London SE1 3HA

ISBN: 978-1-84837-981-7
AD001808EN

Printed in the UK

ALLEN CARR

What the media say about
Allen Carr's Easyway

'I was exhilarated by a new sense of freedom.'
The Independent

'A different approach. A stunning success.'
The Sun

'His skill is in removing the psychological dependence.'
Sunday Times

'Allow Allen Carr to help you escape today.'
The Observer

'An intelligent and original method!'
London Evening Standard

'For the first time in my adult life I am free.'
Woman's Journal

'I reckon this method is as close to foolproof as it gets.'
Time Out

'The Allen Carr method is totally unique in its approach.'
GQ magazine

Allen Carr's Easyway

The key that will set you free

CONTENTS

Introduction 10

Chapter 1 *The Key* 13

Chapter 2 *Choose Happiness* 26

Chapter 3 *Why You're Reading This Book* 35

Chapter 4 *The Trap* 47

Chapter 5 *Illusions* 64

Chapter 6 *Fear* 81

Chapter 7 *Willpower* 87

Chapter 8 *The Addictive Personality* 99

Chapter 9 *Getting Hooked* 106

Chapter 10 *I'm Not A Spendaholic* 117

Chapter 11 *The Three Essentials* 129

Chapter 12 *The Credit Trap* 144

Chapter 13 *Nothing to Fear* 155

Chapter 14 *Taking Control* 167

Chapter 15 *Making Plans* 176

Chapter 16 *Reduce Your Spending The Easy Way* 194

Chapter 17 *Treating Yourself* 206

Chapter 18 *The Fourth Essential* 216

Chapter 19 *Enjoy Life To The Full* 234

Allen Carr's Easyway Clinics 242

INTRODUCTION

'Home life ceases to be free and beautiful as soon as it is founded on borrowing and debt.'
Henrik Ibsen

Anyone who has been trapped in debt will know how it can quickly turn us from happy, confident, positive people into miserable, insecure wrecks. Money wields tremendous power and when you find yourself on the wrong end of that power it can be very intimidating.

One of the reasons why so many people remain in debt is that we are led to believe there is only one way out: the hard way. We've been given the impression that it can't be done without suffering and deprivation and the way governments have recently gone about trying to tackle their own debt crises has reinforced this fear. But I have good news for you, **THERE IS ANOTHER WAY**.

In 1989 I had a remarkable experience. I went to Allen Carr's clinic in the hope that he could help me stop smoking and to my amazement I succeeded easily, painlessly and permanently. It was a completely different experience to my previous attempts to quit by using willpower and nicotine gum. This time I had no desire to smoke so didn't need willpower. I immediately started enjoying social occasions more and handling stress better. There was no feeling of deprivation, instead I felt hugely relieved and elated that I was finally free. I was so impressed with Allen Carr's method that I wrote to him asking if I could join his mission to cure the world of smoking. I was lucky enough to be accepted, and even luckier later to be appointed Managing Director of the company formed to spread the method all over the world.

Today over 400,000 people have visited our clinics in more than 45 countries around the world, and Allen Carr's books have sold over 14 million copies, been translated into more than 40 languages and read by an estimated 30-40 million people. This phenomenal success has been achieved through the personal recommendations of the millions of people who, like me, have succeeded with the method. Allen Carr's Easyway has spread all over the world for one reason alone: **BECAUSE IT WORKS**.

Before I fell into the nicotine trap, I already had another problem. I was overweight. Until the age of 35 I fought a continuous battle to keep my weight down, trying all sorts of diets and constantly using willpower. For over 20 years my weight went up and down depending on whether I was following a diet or indulging myself. I was so unhappy with my body and so miserable that I couldn't solve the problem that it eventually affected me psychologically and I suffered from various eating disorders. That all changed when Allen showed me his first draft of *Allen Carr's Easyweigh to Lose Weight* and I realised he had found the solution to the problem that had plagued my whole life. As I read through the text, I found the powerful logic irrefutable. By the end, I knew that my weight problem was solved.

Until then I had been unsure whether Allen's method could be successfully applied to problems beyond the obvious addictions: smoking, alcoholism, drug abuse. Now I had no doubts.

Get Out of Debt Now applies Allen Carr's Easyway method

to one of the most widespread problems of all. Like smoking, alcoholism and over-eating, debt can have a devastating effect on our life and personality. It can destroy our self-confidence and make us defensive, secretive and hard to reach. Enslaved by debt, we withdraw into our own private world of suffering and we fear that escape is impossible. Ironically, while millions of people are experiencing the same misery all around us, we feel as if we're alone.

Get Out of Debt Now is the key that will set you free from this prison. It will strip away all the illusions and fears that are preventing you from escaping the trap and completely change your mindset, so that you will be able to look forward to enjoying the rest of your life free from the debilitating burden of financial stress.

Regardless of how much money you have, not owing anything to your bank, the credit cards companies, loan sharks or your family or friends will bring you a marvellous sense of wellbeing. Once you are in the right frame of mind, following the practical steps set out in this book to solve your problem will become easy.

Get Out of Debt Now presents Allen Carr's Easyway method in a new, highly accessible format and it will help you to escape the misery of debt without suffering and without sacrifice.

Allen Carr's Easyway can transform your life in the same fantastic way that it has transformed mine.

Robin Hayley M.A. (Oxon), M.B.A., M.A.A.C.T.I.
Managing Director, Allen Carr's Easyway (International) Ltd

CHAPTER 1

THE KEY

IN THIS CHAPTER
• *THE AIM OF THIS BOOK* • *A PRIVATE MATTER*
• *ADDICTION AND THE ALLEN CARR METHOD* • *YOU ARE NOT ALONE*
• *THE DESIRE TO OVER-SPEND* • *HAPPINESS STARTS HERE*

Buy everything you need and lead a rich and fulfilling life, while clearing all your debts and rebuilding your relationships, without using willpower or feeling any sense of deprivation or sacrifice.

Does that strike you as an impossible dream? I promise you it is achievable, regardless of who you are or your personal circumstances. All you need is an open mind.

By reading this book, you will discover a wonderful new life that will bring you a sense of wellbeing that you had forgotten even existed. You will regain control over your finances, you will derive genuine pleasure from the money you spend and you will be free from the crippling worry of debt. And what's more, you'll find it easy.

Perhaps that sounds just too good to be true. Perhaps it contradicts everything you've ever been told up until now about money and debt. But has what you've been told before actually worked for you? If it had, you wouldn't be reading this book.

There's no need for you to be miserable. On the contrary, the main aim of this book is to help you escape the misery of debt and regain the happiness of being free from financial anxiety. There's nothing wrong with spending money provided you are the one in control. Right now, you are not in control and your spending is dragging you deeper and deeper into misery.

A PRIVATE MATTER

Debt is a very lonely condition. It can afflict anyone – jobless or high earner, young or old. Although millions of people are suffering the misery of debt right now, the feeling is one of isolation.

No one likes to talk about their money problems. Their pride is at stake, in addition to which people in debt have a tendency to think there's something unique about their own situation that only they can resolve.

This book is the best friend you could have to help you solve your debt problem. It will not judge you or embarrass you. It will not put pressure on you to undergo painful measures. However, it will help you to understand every aspect of your predicament and enable you to follow a tried and tested method that will lead you out of debt.

You are not alone and your debt problem is not a consequence of your personality. Regardless of your background and current circumstances, this book will help you escape the suffering of debt: the daily fear of financial demands that you cannot meet; the nagging loss of self-confidence; the enforced secrecy and dishonesty; the anger and defensiveness.

In order to get out of debt, you need first of all to take on board the exact nature of the problem and then to follow an effective method to resolve it.

This book will enable you to do both things by applying to your debt problem the most successful system ever designed for overcoming addiction.

DID YOU SAY ADDICTION?

That's right. At this point I should clarify the type of debt we are concerned with. Debt's a word we've often heard in recent years. Banks, businesses and countries are in debt to the tune of billions of pounds. Businessmen deal with debt all the time. We are not concerned with that type of debt here.

This book is aimed at anyone who is suffering the torment of debt at a personal level as a result of over-spending.

Clearly, if you spend more than you have, you will go into debt. Over-spending causes the daily suffering of millions of people all around the world.

Feeling unable to stop over-spending despite being in debt is a form of addiction. You've probably heard the expression 'shopaholic' and dismissed it as a humorous term for someone with a weakness for spending. It probably never occurred to you that there might really be a connection between debt and alcoholism. Well, there is.

As with universally recognised addictions such as smoking, alcoholism and other forms of drug abuse, it's the illusion that the behaviour provides a genuine pleasure or crutch that keeps you trapped. Smokers suffer the illusion that cigarettes help them relax. In fact, they do the complete opposite. All a cigarette does is partially and temporarily relieve the unrelaxing feeling of the body withdrawing from nicotine which non-smokers do not suffer from in the first place. It's like putting on tight shoes just for the relief of taking them off.

As the nicotine leaves the body, smokers start to feel uptight and unfortunately they're under the illusion that the only thing that will make them feel better is another cigarette. The reality is that the next cigarette will simply introduce more nicotine into the body, guaranteeing that, when that nicotine leaves, the smoker will again become uptight and feel the urge for another cigarette. Non-smokers do not have this problem.

SMOKERS, THEREFORE, SMOKE IN ORDER TO FEEL LIKE NON-SMOKERS

The same mechanism is at work when it comes to over-spending. The illusion is that over-spending makes you feel good. In fact, all it's doing is giving you a momentary taste of how someone without debt feels all the time. While you're over-spending, you manage to block from your mind the fact that you can't afford what you're buying, and so for that brief moment you feel the sense of freedom and confidence that someone who is not in debt feels all the time. However, that boost soon wears off and you're left feeling miserable again and guilty that now you're in even more debt. However, because you think the only thing that can make you feel better is to spend, you go and spend more.

Instead of removing your misery by getting rid of your debt, you increase the debt, thus ensuring that the misery gets worse. The longer you go on labouring under the illusion that over-spending gives you a pleasure or a crutch, the further you will descend into the debt trap and the more miserable you will become.

Jan's story is a stark example of how the illusion of pleasure can blind us to reality and lead to severe debt problems.

JAN'S STORY

Jan lives with her son, Ted, in a suburb of Edinburgh. Ted is 26, has been diagnosed with a mildly debilitating illness, doesn't work and spends all day playing games on the internet. He plagues his mother with phone calls at work, asking her to get this DVD, that CD, or bring him home something from the bakery. He has even been known to text his mother to come upstairs to the bedroom, then ask her to change the channel on his TV. He is overweight and virtually housebound, and he puts all his problems down to the effects of his illness.

A few years ago, Ted had a credit card and ran up a big debt. Fortunately, a friend of his mother's gave him some good financial advice and he managed to pay back what he owed. Now he doesn't have a credit card, but Jan does.

She started off with a limit of £2,000 and soon spent her way up to that total, paying off the minimum each month. No problem, she got another card offering 0% for a year with a limit of £5,000, meaning she could transfer the £2,000 debt on to that card and have another £3,000 to spend. And so it went on.

She now owes £15,000 on one card and about £6,000 on others. Nearly all of that money has gone on buying things for Ted, in the hope that it will make him happy. All the latest gadgets, phones, computers etc, expensive sunglasses (which he hardly uses as he seldom leaves the house), a large pedigree dog, which had to be rehomed after a few weeks because Ted was incapable of looking after it, and a whole host of other unnecessary items. She takes Ted and her husband, Ken, away on holiday three times a year and last summer she spent £600 on a holiday for Ted in Turkey with some friends, only for him to return home after one day, at more expense to his mother.

Jan doesn't earn a lot of money and has no plan to pay off her debts. Her friends have given up trying to give her advice. Now she is doing the usual dodging of phone calls and not answering letters. Although her debts are piling up, she says she wouldn't give up her credit cards under any circumstances; her life would be nothing without them.

Jan's story may strike you as extreme, but it's typical of the way we fall into the debt trap. Many people will look at Jan's situation and say, 'The problem's not Jan, it's Ted. She needs to stop spoiling him and get him to sort his life out.'

What if I told you the same applies to you? Perhaps you don't have a Ted in your life, or you think you don't. In fact, you do; we all do. If you think of Ted as the side of all of us that takes a fancy to things and wants to own them, you can begin to relate more closely to Jan's story.

Jan knows that if Ted is happy, she's happy, and she believes she can make Ted happy by spending money on him. Anyone looking at her situation can clearly see that that is the last thing she should be doing. But Jan is so wrapped up in the fog of spending addiction that she cannot see any solution to her debt problem and sees no alternative but to continue over-spending.

Now look at your own situation. Isn't it the case that you try to achieve happiness by spending money on your inner Ted? This book will help you unravel the illusions that trap you in debt. It will help you to see that spending does not relieve your misery, it is the cause of it.

The misery of debt is one of the most devastating conditions known to man and it is an entirely man-made problem. As with all addictions, it starts small, seemingly under control, but it soon grows to the point where it takes you over. You find yourself in debt and as your creditors demand repayment, the only way you can see to keep them at bay is to bury yourself in more debt by borrowing from someone else. You would love to pay it all off but your outgoings exceed your income, so there's no spare money to do so. In fact, you're going deeper and deeper into debt each month and you just can't see a way out.

Once you recognise that over-spending is an addiction, you can begin your escape. That was the revelation that triggered this book. I was one of the worst nicotine addicts you could ever meet, a chain-smoker who choked his way through 100 cigarettes a day and was resigned to an early death. I was under the misapprehension that smoking was a habit I had acquired and that I lacked the willpower to quit. My revelation came when I realised that smoking was an addiction.

In that moment the fog lifted from my mind and I saw with extraordinary clarity that the problem was neither some weakness in my character, nor was it some magical quality of the cigarette. Once I understood how the addiction worked, it was clear to me that smoking provided no genuine pleasure or crutch and therefore that stopping involved no sacrifice or deprivation. I quit there and then and started my mission to help the world's smokers do the same.

I called the method Easyway. It requires no willpower, no substitutes, no gimmicks, no nicotine products. It simply enables smokers to become happy non-smokers by unravelling the brainwashing that convinced them that smoking was a pleasure or a crutch. Once the illusion that they are making a sacrifice by stopping has been removed, they find it easy to quit because they don't feel deprived and they are happy to be free.

I knew this method would work for all addictions and it has already been successfully applied to alcohol, other drugs and over-eating. Now we are applying it to one of the most debilitating problems of all: debt.

YOU ARE NOT ALONE

Perhaps you still find it hard to accept that your over-spending is an addiction like smoking. This book will explain to you why it is exactly that. Debt grips hold of you and traps you in a prison of illusions in the same way that nicotine traps smokers, alcohol traps alcoholics and heroin traps junkies. If you can appreciate the masochism of the heroin addict every time they stick a needle into their arm, by the time you've read this book, you will be able to appreciate the masochism of the borrower every time they incur more debt. Over-spending is destroying your life and the only way to change that is to stop doing it.

At this stage it doesn't matter whether you believe me or not. All I ask is that you keep an open mind. Once you recognise that over-spending is an addiction that provides you with no genuine pleasure or crutch, you will see that there is nothing particular about you that has landed you in this predicament and you will be able to escape easily and painlessly.

Perhaps you consider yourself low paid and, therefore more vulnerable to debt than most. Well, many highly paid people have debt problems too. In fact, the highly paid often go more heavily into debt than the low paid, which means the problem is scaled up and so are the consequences.

Perhaps, deep down, you feel that there's something within your personality that makes you vulnerable to debt and incapable of getting out of it. Dismiss any such thoughts from your mind right now!

The world is full of people suffering the agony of debt and most of them are suffering in silence. Even before the global financial collapse of 2008, a third of the adult population of the so-called First World was in debt. Why, in a society that has all it needs, do millions of people continue to suffer from debt?

The answer is simple: because debt involves an addiction that, like all addictions, traps addicts in a downward spiral from which they don't know how to escape.

Please don't fool yourself into thinking that because so many people are in debt, it must be OK. There is no safety in numbers here. The ill effects of debt prey on us all individually, eating away at our quality of life. The fact that millions of others are experiencing the same suffering does not lessen its impact on you. You don't like being in debt, that's why you're reading this book.

The real cause of Jan's debt problem is the belief that spending money will alleviate the other difficulties in her life, when in reality it is simply creating more misery. Later you will read the accounts of other people, each of whom fell into severe debt through different circumstances. You may well recognise yourself in their stories. While the background to their debt problems may differ, the debt problem itself and the way to solve it are the same in every case.

Whoever you are, whatever you do, wherever you live, however much you earn, you can find yourself enslaved by money misery. The good news is that you can also get out of debt easily, painlessly and permanently. All you have to do is read this book and follow all the instructions.

CONTROL

Like all addicts, people with debt problems try to kid themselves and others that they're in control, even when it's blatantly obvious that they're not. There's nothing more pathetic than the person who buries their head in the sand, shoves bills unopened in a drawer and continues to hammer their credit cards in order to try to avoid confronting the full horror of their situation at any cost.

This is another of the illusions that keeps us trapped. It's like a driver trying to control a car that's skidding on ice. They can wrestle with the wheel all they like, but the car won't be able to alter its course. They're on the skids, and the only way to stop is to get off the ice.

Get it clearly into your mind, if you have a debt problem, you are not in control. Your credit card does not give you power, it gives the credit company power over you. An overdraft facility does not give you control of how much you spend, it gives the bank control over you.

The big question is why do we even think that spending money will make us happy in the first place?

The answer is because that is what we are brainwashed to believe from childhood.

From the moment we are old enough to understand the exchange of money for goods, we are led to believe that spending leads to happiness. This illusion is shamelessly exploited by what I call Big Retail.

By that I mean everyone with a vested interest in selling goods, from retailers to advertisers. Indeed the advertising industry exists for the sole purpose of creating illusions linking products to happiness.

It's virtually impossible to go through a single day – or even a single minute if you're surfing the internet – without someone trying to sell you something you don't need. It's a pity there's no organization whose job it is to unravel the lies and the brainwashing of Big Retail, no advertising industry that exists solely to tell us the truth about all these unnecessary goods.

We're so taken in by Big Retail that even when we sense that our over-spending is causing us misery, we still continue to do it, plunging ourselves deeper and deeper into debt. The good news is that once you can see through the brainwashing and understand the nature of the trap, you will no longer be conned into thinking that spending makes you feel better and you will find it easy to escape.

FREEDOM STARTS HERE

This book will give you all the help you need to dissolve the illusions that have kept you trapped. You now hold the key to your own prison. Remember, whatever methods you may have tried to get out of debt before have not worked. So dismiss all the misinformation you've been fed until now and free your mind to follow a method that has already enabled millions of people to escape from slavery.

So let's start the process now. You will soon be able to enjoy the happiness that freedom will bring.

SUMMARY

- Whatever you've been told about debt up until now hasn't worked for you, so ignore it.

- There is nothing particular to you or your circumstances that means you have to live your life in debt.

- Over-spending is an addiction.

- Addiction feeds on illusions.

- The belief that spending equals pleasure is an illusion created by Big Retail.

- Keep an open mind and getting out of debt will be easy.

Chapter 2

CHOOSE HAPPINESS

> ## IN THIS CHAPTER
> - *PERCEPTION – A MATTER OF CHOICE*
> - *CONFIDENCE V WORRY*
> - *ESCAPING THE VICIOUS CIRCLE*

The misery of debt is a state of mind that can be easily reversed.

It's early on a Saturday morning in May – my favourite month. The sun is up and as I raise the blinds it floods into my room, bringing a radiance to every surface. I can see pollen suspended in the streams of light and outside a soft blanket of mist hovers above the grass, drawn from the earth in a fine steam by the sun's warming rays.

Fresh from a good night's sleep, I prepare a healthy breakfast of fruit and think what I might do with this fine day. The phone rings and I reach for the receiver with a sense of anticipation. It's my friend Matthew. Today is his birthday. Do I fancy a round of golf, followed by watching the football in the pub and then meeting up with our other halves and trying that new restaurant that's just opened in town? My spirits soar. I couldn't think of anything better.

I take a shower, put on some comfortable clothes, check that there are plenty of balls in my golf bag, wash up the breakfast things and sit by the window reading a book until I hear Matthew's car pull up outside.

It's a beautiful day for golf, even if my own game doesn't exactly do justice to the occasion. The round costs me £20 and I enjoy every penny spent. I buy Matthew lunch in the clubhouse as a 'thank you' for driving me – another £20 – and then we drive back to my house, where he parks and we walk to the pub. A few other friends are there for the match and we put £10 each into the drinks kitty. We all enjoy a raucous couple of hours watching the football before heading home to wash, change and meet our partners.

The restaurant is a roaring success. The food is superb, the ambience lively and relaxed and the price very reasonable: £30 per head. Matt and I settle the bill between us and we all stroll back home, enjoying the gentle breeze of a warm early summer evening. By the time I climb into bed, I'm ready to sleep. I cast my mind back over the events of the day with total fulfilment and as my head touches the pillow I feel myself slipping effortlessly into a delicious, contented sleep.

If I were asked to describe my dream day, this is more or less how it goes. Some of the details might change. Instead of playing golf I might go fishing by a sparkling stream at the bottom of a lush meadow, with a picnic and a cool drink suspended in the water from a string tied to a branch. But the essence and the emotions of the dream are always the same. I'm happy to say I have experienced days just like this. But there was a time when the prospect of such a day as I have described was a nightmare. It would go like this:

The sun forcing its way past the blinds wakes me early from a restless sleep and I lie in bed, my muscles tense, my brain whirring with a thousand different thoughts. Unable to get back to sleep, I get up, go to the kitchen and try to comfort myself with a stack of buttered toast. As I eat I pace the room, bracing myself against the negative thoughts that are queuing up to plague my mind and trying to put all my obligations into some order of priority.

The phone rings and I jump, startled. Then I swear. Who on earth is ringing me at this time on a Saturday morning and what the heck do they want? I let the answer machine get it. Matthew leaves a message inviting me to play golf, followed by an afternoon in the pub watching football and an evening meal at the new restaurant in town. The suggestion frightens me. Golf will cost me £20. An afternoon in the pub will be another tenner and then who knows what they charge in that new restaurant. I've heard it's good but it's bound to set me back a few quid. I'm probably looking at £60 for the day if I'm lucky.

I call Matt back and tell him I'll have to pass. He reminds me that it's his birthday. Reluctantly, I agree to go along with his plan.

I try to take a shower but there's something wrong with the thing and I spend five minutes being alternately frozen then scalded by a puny trickle of water. I pull out some clothes that might pass as golf attire, but they feel tight and shabby and make me look depressingly old-fashioned. I'm already feeling resentful by the time Matthew pulls up and honks his horn.

At the golf club I hand over my £20, the only note I have in my wallet, and try to forget about it. I play appallingly and lose my temper a couple of times. Matthew suggests we have a spot of lunch at the club before heading back to town, so I choose a sandwich, which I pay for with my credit card. I don't offer to buy Matthew's, though I feel I should, and I'm still feeling a bit guilty when we arrive at the pub. To make matters worse, there are some other friends there and they ask for £10 each towards the drinks kitty. I tell them I haven't got any cash and ask if I can use my card. They wave it away with a laugh and tell me I can owe it to them, but I feel so bad about it that I spend the afternoon buying my own drinks with my card and feeling like an outcast. They're all laughing and joking but all I can think about is how I'm going to make up for the money I've already spent.

By the time we reach the restaurant Matthew has picked up on my stress and the mood can best be described as despondent. Poor guy. It's supposed to be his birthday and I've brought him down. I try to relax during the meal but all I can think about is the price of everything and I find myself criticizing it all, from the size of the portions to the speed of the service. Paying the bill is agony. This is money I can ill afford to spend on something as unnecessary as a meal out. I could have used it to pay one of the instalments on that vacuum cleaner I had to buy when the old one broke down. I put my card in the machine and choose the No Tip option.

I walk home in silence, my head bowed. I bid farewell to Matthew, offer him a strained 'Happy Birthday' (I'm sure it would have been had it not been for me) and close the door. I'm alone. I should go to bed but I don't feel ready. My brain is whirring again, reflecting on the money I've spent today and for what? A terrible round of golf, a miserable afternoon in the pub and a meal that didn't even fill me up. Tomorrow's Sunday: a day of nothingness with nothing to look forward to but a new working week.

I turn the TV on and watch inane rubbish until 2am. Then I drag myself to bed and lie awake until 3am, when finally the gyroscope in my head stops spinning.

I have had days like this, when nothing could give me pleasure. People in debt have the same problem all the time: they are so plagued with money worries that they can no longer find the pleasure in what were once their favourite pastimes, and they allow their basic lifestyle to become uncomfortable and irritating.

If they could see that the difference between the dream and the nightmare is a simple matter of perception, they would solve their problem there and then. But when you're in the grip of debt you're a slave to money and you can only see life one way: through negative eyes.

But you have in your hands the way out of this prison. All you have to do is use it. As you progress through the book, I will give you all the instructions you need to get free, starting now:

FIRST INSTRUCTION:

FOLLOW ALL THE INSTRUCTIONS

Perhaps you think this is my idea of a joke. It's not, I'm being serious. This method will enable you to solve your debt problem with ease, but the method only works if you follow ALL the instructions. Say I give you the combination to a safe. It consists of a series of numbers, which you have to enter in the correct order. If you leave out any of the numbers, or try to use them in the wrong order, the safe will remain locked. This method works in the same way. You are going to be given the instructions that will unlock the door of your financial prison. Follow each one in order and the lock will spring open.

HAPPINESS

When you're in the debt trap, it can seem tempting to resign yourself to your miserable fate. **PUT THAT THOUGHT OUT OF YOUR MIND RIGHT NOW!**

Every human being has the potential to be happy – including you. There is nothing that dictates that some people will be happy and some will be miserable. In fact, happiness is largely a matter of personal choice.

Perhaps you think that's ridiculously simplistic. Human beings have always had the capacity to inflict misery on others. How can I tell someone who's in a terrible financial mess that it's up to them whether they choose to be happy or not?

It's not my place to tell anyone how they should feel. But there are countless people who have remained positive and optimistic in the direst of circumstances. A prime example is Nelson Mandela. Despite being imprisoned in South Africa for 27 years, he refused to be demoralised and remained optimistic that the fight against apartheid and for equality he had been so involved in on the outside would be won. He continued to be an inspiration to the cause and on his release became president of his country. Mandela could have crumbled. He could have given up, resigned himself to his life sentence and departed this world unnoticed. Instead, he chose the alternative path. Mandela refused to give in to his circumstances, even though it must have been very difficult to see a way out.

Up until now you may have feared that you would never be able to get out of the misery of debt. That's because up until now you've been going about it the wrong way. Get it clearly into your mind, escape is not only possible but certain, provided you understand this book and follow the instructions. Fortunately, unlike Mandela, you are not in a physical prison and you are your own jailer. So cast aside any feelings of doom or gloom and look forward to enjoying life free from the anxiety of financial stress. That way happiness lies.

IF YOU FOLLOW THE ADVICE IN THIS BOOK YOU WILL END THE MISERY OF DEBT AND OPEN THE DOOR TO HAPPINESS

If you think you're condemned to a life of money worries, think again. After reading this book you will see that you can not only be debt-free but also regain your energy, enthusiasm, confidence, self-respect and pleasure in life.

A setback like losing your job or getting divorced can drain your confidence. Worrying about money certainly does. The more we worry, the less confident we feel; and the less confident we feel, the more we worry. It's a vicious circle. But it can be escaped from. Start to build your confidence again and your worries reduce. As your worries reduce, your confidence grows.

We all want success and happiness. You won't find it by living beyond your means. That's a recipe for failure and misery. You are about to end the vicious circle.

I said you are holding the key to your prison in your hands and all you have to do is use it. Fine, so why don't I just tell you the secret immediately so that you can get free now? Don't worry, you will be free very soon. The method is not a secret; it works rather like the combination of a safe. You have to understand each point as I explain it to you – if you only use part of it or apply it in the wrong order, it won't work. If you only read part of this book, you will not acquire a proper understanding of the method.

REMEMBER: THIS METHOD WILL ENABLE YOU TO REGAIN CONTROL OF YOUR FINANCES WITHOUT USING WILLPOWER OR FEELING ANY SENSE OF DEPRIVATION OR SACRIFICE. YOU WILL BE ABLE TO BUY EVERYTHING YOU NEED AND LEAD A RICH AND FULFILLING LIFE, WHILE CLEARING YOUR DEBTS, AND REBUILDING YOUR RELATIONSHIPS, MAKING YOU HAPPIER THAN YOU CAN IMAGINE

Perhaps you still find that hard to believe. Don't worry. All I ask is that you remain open to all possibilities. Whether you believe me or not at this stage has no bearing on whether the method will work for you. Provided that the correct numbers are used in the correct order, a combination lock opens regardless of whether the person putting in the numbers believes it will. As long as you follow the method, it will work.

And as you begin to see it working, your confidence will begin to grow. Then you will begin to believe, and that in turn will help to transform the vicious circle into a virtuous one.

Just keep an open mind and follow the method.

SUMMARY

- This book is the key to your prison – all you have to do is use it.
- First instruction: follow all the instructions.
- You have the chance to be happy – take it.
- Restore your confidence and your worries will dissolve.
- Second instruction: keep an open mind.

Chapter 3

WHY YOU'RE READING THIS BOOK

IN THIS CHAPTER
•*FEAR* •*THE IMPRESSIONABLE MIND* •*WHY WE GET INTO DEBT*
•*THE ROOT OF ALL EVIL* •*SIGNS OF HAVING LOST CONTROL*
•*FACING UP TO THE SCALE OF THE PROBLEM*

*We are enslaved by our perception of the power of money.
Breaking free is easy with the right frame of mind.*

THE GREAT TABOO

When I was young I asked my mother how much a wealthy friend of my parents earned, and was told that you don't ask questions like that. I still have no idea what most of my friends earn. I certainly don't know what level of debt any of them might be in, and when I had my own money troubles I didn't tell them either.

We're meant to be able to share our worries with our friends and turn to them for moral support. But a debt problem makes you feel as if you're a failure and involves a loss of face, so it's difficult to share it with others. This can lead to an awful feeling of isolation.

You don't have to be on a low income to find yourself in debt.

*'Annual income twenty pounds, annual expenditure nineteen
and six, result happiness. Annual income twenty pounds,
annual expenditure twenty pounds ought and six, result misery.'*
- Mr Micawber,
(*David Copperfield* by Charles Dickens)

IN HIS OWN WORDS: DAVID

I had a fairly well-paid job and always received my salary on time every month. It should have been fairly easy for me to keep my head above water. But somehow I got so heavily into debt that my wages were swallowed up within a few days, leaving me most of the month to flounder around, trying to keep my life from crashing on the rocks.

It didn't stop me spending, though. On the contrary, the idea of accumulating goods gave me a momentary sense of relief – that was, until the money was spent. The anticipation I felt before a shopping spree was never matched by any sense of satisfaction afterwards. Rather, I felt as if I'd let myself down again. I felt foolish and ashamed. No one else seemed to be having the problems I was having.

David concluded that there must be something wrong with him, something lacking. He felt a failure.

Why a failure? Because he was labouring under the common misconception that money equals success. We look at the trappings of wealth and we equate them with all that we admire in life:

Respect

Choice

Power

Confidence

Freedom

Happiness

Ease

Success

From the moment we are born we are bombarded with mixed messages about money:

We hear that: 'The love of money is the root of all evil.' On the other hand we're also told: 'Money makes the world go round.'

These days, the power of celebrity has further intensified the illusion that money equals success. It's hard to go anywhere without seeing some airbrushed star beaming down at you from a billboard, looking happy and relaxed, as if all the woes that plague your life have no place in theirs.

It's an illusion, of course, but we don't see it that way. We want to believe in the fantasy, so we take it at face value. The natural reaction is to crave what they appear to have: money, beauty, glamour, luxury, excitement. We put two and two together and conclude that spending is the way to happiness. So we spend and at that moment we do get an initial boost as it gives us a feeling of power and control. However, that boost quickly wears off and we find that, far from leaving us fulfilled, we again feel in need of another boost, so we spend again.

This cycle then repeats itself over and over again. All the time we're sinking further and further into the abyss of debt, our quality of life is getting worse and worse and we're getting more and more desperate. Ironically, the further we slide into the pit, the more we feel in need of the little boost and the more we turn to spending.

This is how addiction works. It turns reality on its head. It creates a problem and makes us seek a solution by doing the very thing that's causing the problem in the first place.

THE MORE WE SEEK HAPPINESS THROUGH SPENDING, THE MORE DESPERATE AND MISERABLE IT MAKES US FEEL

You're reading this book because you've realised something is wrong. That's a major step you've taken. Something you thought would make you happy is making you miserable and you've decided to do something about it. Good for you. You've already started the process of solving your problem and, provided you understand the method and follow the instructions, nothing can prevent you from succeeding.

MIXED MESSAGES

'I am opposed to millionaires, but it would be dangerous to offer me the position.'
Mark Twain

DELIGHT

'Money makes the world go round,
In for a penny, in for a pound.'

DISGUST

'The love of money is the root of all evil.'
'Money-grabbing gold-diggers…'
'Filthy lucre…'
'It is easier for a camel to go through the eye of a needle than for a rich man to enter the kingdom of God.'

CAUTION

'A fool and his money are soon parted.'
'Take care of the pennies and the pounds will take care of themselves.'
'Penny wise, pound foolish…'
'Money doesn't grow on trees.'

Some of these sayings encourage you to keep a careful hold of your money, others encourage you to get rid of it. Some suggest that money is of huge importance, others take the moral high ground and judge you for showing too much interest in it. Society's attitude to money is very confusing. To spend or not to spend? We abhor meanness and hoarding, and applaud generosity. At the same time we admire financial prudence and despise ostentation. We also confuse generosity with extravagance.

I've come across people, including those in debt, who feel as if they've failed if they leave a shop empty-handed. Often they squander money on tat just for the sake of it.

THE FACT IS THAT BOTH EXTREMES, THE MISER AND THE SPENDTHRIFT, ARE LABOURING UNDER THE SAME MISCONCEPTION: THAT MONEY IS OF PARAMOUNT IMPORTANCE, A SURE SIGN OF SUCCESS. THEY, THEREFORE, ALLOW IT TO DOMINATE THEIR LIVES

Both are deluded. A successful life is a contented one, and true contentment can only be achieved when you see money for what it really is – simply a means to an end.

Money is just a medium that gives you more freedom in the market than if you were only able to exchange goods through barter.

SECOND INSTRUCTION:
KEEP AN OPEN MIND

This is the second in the series of instructions that, provided you follow them all, will lead you out of debt and into a new, happy way of life. You may already regard yourself as an open-minded person, willing to try anything once. What I'm talking about goes deeper than that. The fact is that we go through life with our minds largely made up. For example, when you see the sun rise in the morning you interpret it as a ball of fiery gases burning millions of miles away. It has the appearance of rising in the sky because the Earth is spinning. How do you know that's the case? Because you've been presented with some very convincing arguments by people in the know.

If I were to tell you it's actually God driving a fiery chariot across the sky, you'd think I'd lost my marbles.

What do you see below? A square table and a rectangular one?

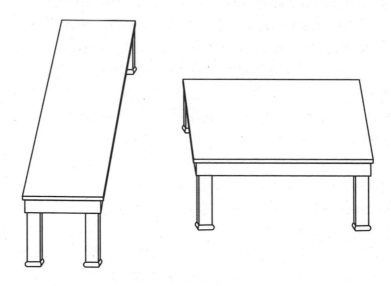

You've accepted that it's one square table and one rectangular one because that's what it looks like and I've suggested it is. Now if I were to tell you that the dimensions of each table are exactly the same, would you believe me? I think not. However, I assure you they are. Take a ruler and measure them. Extraordinary, isn't it!

The point is that our minds can be easily tricked into accepting as true something that is false.

Whenever David went on a 'retail therapy' spree, another delusion was in play: that he was spending of his own free will. It didn't even cross his mind that he wasn't. After all, nobody was holding a gun to his head. It was his choice.

But what if you're basing your choice on false beliefs?

This is why I want you to remember the diagram of the tables and keep an open mind, so that even if I tell you something that you find difficult to believe, you will accept the possibility that what I say is true.

WHY WE GET INTO DEBT

Big Retail constantly bombards us with messages that buying things will make us happy. In fact, over-spending makes you miserable. If you spend more than you have, you'll get into debt. Whether you do it to the tune of £50 or £50,000, the principle is the same. Whether you earn a meagre wage or you're a millionaire, if you spend more than you have and cannot pay it off, the debt is only going to do one thing: grow.

You may think you're in control but actually you're being controlled by an addiction. The delusion that you can buy happiness drives you to spend more than you have, which in reality leads to misery. The more you try to find happiness by over-spending, the deeper into debt you plunge and the more miserable you become.

If your debts were no problem, you wouldn't be reading this book. There are some classic signs that the situation is beginning to get out of control:

- You start missing payments, e.g. on a credit card
- You avoid opening bills
- You avoid friends and family members who have lent you money
- You stop spending money on genuine pleasures like recreation and entertainment
- You lie about your financial situation.

Any of these actions point to the fact that your debts are controlling you. Fortunately this situation can be easily reversed once your perceptions have changed and that's what this book is all about.

FACE UP TO THE PROBLEM

Later I will explain a system by which you can calmly look at the actual extent of your debt problem. For now, enjoy thinking about the fact that by the time you finish this book you will have found a practical way to deal with your debts without anxiety or constant evasion tactics.

The ability to avoid payment can become a strange source of personal pride. Juggling your debts between credit cards and persuading your bank manager that a big cheque is in the post and will solve your overdraft becomes a game, a bit like gambling. You're getting one over on the fat cats.

THE TRUTH IS YOU'RE NOT GETTING ONE OVER ON ANYBODY EXCEPT YOURSELF. THE MORE YOU PROLONG THE SITUATION, THE MORE THE FAT CATS WILL SQUEEZE YOU

As long as you remain in debt, you will not be free. Your debt will control you. One of the great joys of being debt-free is not having to deal with creditors, whom you regard as the enemy. Right now you know they're exploiting you, but you think you need them, so you play along. Meanwhile, they are laughing all the way to the bank, raking in extra interest and dumping extra charges on your monthly bill.

Denial is a common trait amongst those in debt. Some people will do virtually anything in their power to keep the truth from others, and worse, they will also deny the truth to themselves. That's because accepting that we have a debt problem can make us feel foolish and ashamed, a failure.

BEING IN DEBT DOESN'T MEAN YOU ARE A FAILURE

The fact that debt afflicts so many people is, in fact, a failure of the world we live in, a world in which Big Retail is free to brainwash us into believing we need to spend, spend, spend in order to be fulfilled and in which financial institutions are free to behave irresponsibly and encourage people to get into debt – and have often gone to great lengths to do so. You have been trapped. The good news is that you can walk out of that trap any time you want.

You have accepted that you have a debt problem. You have sought help in solving that problem. You are committed to following all the instructions and to keeping an open mind. When you finish this book you will be free from the misery of money worries. Take that on board and enjoy the feeling it gives you.

THIRD INSTRUCTION:
BEGIN WITH A FEELING OF ELATION

It's time to start banishing anxiety from your mind. I promise there's nothing to fear. I have only good news for you. You are taking control and the process is absolutely painless.

You are replacing something that has been making you unspeakably miserable with something that will make you unimaginably happy.

It's a life-changing shift. You don't have to wait until all your debts are cleared before you begin to feel the excitement of what you are about to achieve. The good times start the moment you stop incurring new debts.

'Before borrowing money from a friend, decide which you need most.'
American proverb

SUMMARY

- Being in debt doesn't mean you're a failure.
- Talk, you will find many people share the same problem and even those who don't are sympathetic.
- Face up to the fact you are in debt.
- Don't hide from your creditors.
- Don't spend your time finding ways to avoid your friends.
- The best way to beat your debts is to clear them.

Chapter 4

THE TRAP

IN THIS CHAPTER
• *ADDICTION* • *JUNK-SPENDING* • *THE VOID AND ROLE MODELS*
• *INTELLECT v INSTINCT* • *THE DEBT TRAP*
• *THE TUG OF WAR OF FEAR*

Once you can see the connection between over-spending and other addictions, you can begin to unravel the brainwashing that has lured you into the debt trap.

WHO ARE YOU CALLING AN ADDICT?

All addicts are trapped. The trap works in the same subtle and insidious way with all addictions. So let's look at the relationship between over-spending and various other addictions.

It's easy to understand how smoking is an addiction. Tobacco contains a drug called nicotine, which makes the smoker feel uptight as it leaves the body. If the smoker lights a cigarette during this withdrawal period, they feel more relaxed as the withdrawal is relieved and they are, therefore, fooled into believing they get a genuine pleasure or crutch from smoking. In reality they're just trying to get rid of the empty, insecure feeling of the body withdrawing from nicotine, which non-smokers don't suffer from anyway.

You would be forgiven for assuming that if that's the case, all you need to do to cure the addiction is to remove all the nicotine from the smoker's body. Nicotine is a fast-acting drug that quickly starts to pass out of the bloodstream and leaves the body completely within three days. Surely, therefore, a smoker only needs to survive without a cigarette for three days and the addiction will be cured?

Of course, we all know this isn't the case. Smokers who try to quit by using willpower can go on craving cigarettes for weeks, months, even years after quitting. Some poor souls do so for the rest of their life. This is because they continue to suffer the illusion that smoking gave them a pleasure or a crutch and so they feel deprived.

This is the fundamental point about addiction: the addict is deluded into thinking that salvation lies in the very thing that's causing the misery. The problem may be triggered by the chemical in the body, but it festers and grows in the brain.

Understanding this aspect of addiction enabled my stop smoking method to be applied not only to other recognised addictions such as alcoholism and heroin and cocaine dependency but also to over-eating. I began to understand that addicts are not always addicted to an addictive substance.

Now let's look at debt. Just as we need to eat, we need to spend money to a certain extent. In fact, we need to spend money to eat. The best things in life may well be free, but not everything is. The basics, food, warmth and shelter, cost money. However, we don't just spend money on these essentials. We also spend on a whole host of other items, many of which are not only useless from a practical point of view but also give us no genuine pleasure whatsoever.

I CALL THIS TYPE OF SPENDING 'JUNK-SPENDING'

IN HIS OWN WORDS: SIMON

My life was so good I don't know why I had to go and spoil it. The trouble was, I had a job which involved lots of travel, and perhaps to compensate for spending so much time away from them I began buying expensive presents for my wife and two kids every time I got paid at the end of the month. I wanted to be the perfect dad.

For our tenth wedding anniversary I booked an extravagant holiday in Thailand for all the family. That trip came at a bad time. That's because I had just bought a new car and a combi-boiler to replace one that had blown up. I didn't want to let anybody down, so, finding myself short of cash, I began sticking everything on my credit card. My spending soon spiralled out of control.

The strange thing is that, once you've dipped your toe into debt, it is all too easy to immerse yourself completely. It's so simple putting things on a card; it never feels like letting go of real money. I found myself spending far more now that I was in debt than I had when I was solvent.

Debt increased my feelings of guilt towards my family and, to make up for that, I began buying them more and more expensive presents. I began getting letters from the bank, so I decided to pay off the minimum amount by direct debit each month and everything seemed to be OK for a while. In time, of course, the sum I owed on the card started to balloon and I could hardly believe how much interest I was paying.

For a while I kept my head down, hoping the problem would disappear, but it got worse and worse and I could barely sleep at night for anxiety. I didn't dare tell my wife how irresponsible I'd been. Suddenly I could barely afford to pay household bills any more. Christmas was on its way and I had to work out how I'd pay for some very expensive gifts I'd promised the kids.

There are many reasons why people find themselves in debt. However, once a person has debt problems for whatever reason, certain patterns of behaviour tend to follow. Many people find that even if they are not an habitual over-spender, they try to relieve the misery caused by their condition by spending too much. The boost felt by making a purchase can create a short-lived high that distracts you from your actual problem and at that moment makes you feel as if you don't have the problem.

The act of spending itself makes you feel powerful and confident, as if you have no money worries, and this feels like a great relief from the constant anxiety that otherwise plagues your mind. So, ironically, when you spend in this way, it briefly tricks you into feeling like someone who has no financial problems.

In fact, it makes you feel as you would feel all the time if only you could solve your debt problem. Anyone can be susceptible to junk-spending because Big Retail dresses up junk to seem enticing.

The trouble is, once that temporary relief has subsided, we feel worse than we did before, as the realization that we've wasted more money on pointless products and got further into debt sets in. But because we believe that we get some pleasure or crutch from spending, we mistakenly seek comfort by doing the very thing that's made us miserable in the first place.

THE ADDICTION HAS TAKEN HOLD

Simon initially came to me with his problem because he knew that I used to be an accountant. I said, 'Simon, I can give you some help with your accounts and try to get you back on track, but this is not going to work unless you realise what really makes you happy. You have a beautiful wife and two lovely children, a job you like and a house you own. But if you continue in this way you're likely to lose all those things.

'Your children and wife love you. You don't need to spoil them and try to impress them in this way. You're spending money you don't have on stuff you don't need and, far from making you happy, it's turning your life into a nightmare.

'Cast your mind back to before you started over-spending. Did you feel the need then for all these things you've now bought with borrowed money? Were you feeling deprived?

Compare the quality of life you had then to what you have now. Weren't you happier then?'

Fortunately, Simon had an open mind and was ready to listen to me. After a few hours his mindset had completely changed. We had worked out a failsafe strategy to get him out of debt and he left feeling excited about the future and elated that he had left the misery of being a slave to money behind him. It was that incident which made me realise that my method could be successfully applied to debt and which originally planted the seed for this book.

Consider your debts as the equivalent of the unsightly fat on somebody who is overweight, or as the smoker's cough or the threat of lung cancer. You try to cover them up, you pretend they're not there, you kid yourself that they're under control, you'll deal with them soon, just not yet. But these are growing, dark shadows looming at the back of your mind and as you go further and further into debt, they loom larger and larger, making you more and more miserable.

Can you see the connection now? My method has already helped tens of millions of people to quit smoking, drinking, taking other drugs and over-eating. The same method will help you to get free of debt.

Remember, the fact that you've fallen into the debt trap has nothing to do with your character or personality. Millions of people who have found themselves in the same trap and been convinced that they will never be able to escape have got free and so will you.

I'M NOT A SHOPAHOLIC

Perhaps you think this book is aimed at people who can't resist the temptation to go shopping. That might seem trivial compared to the scale of your debt. You might have lost a fortune in a failed business venture or as a result of some other unhappy event.

The fact is, all debt is caused by the same thing: laying out money you don't have. Whether you're a businessperson who gambles a million pounds on a risky investment (and all investments carry an element of risk), or a student who spends his whole term's money in the first week, you have opened yourself up to debt. If you then fail to address the issue and borrow money in order to carry on, you fall into the same trap.

By spending money you don't have, you're trying to cheat the system. Sure, it's something we're all encouraged to do and it's easy to fall into the trap, but the result is debt. We have only cheated ourselves.

The purpose of this book is not to draw distinctions between the different ways people get into debt, it's to help anyone in debt to get out of it. Regardless of the scale of your debt, it's now an unavoidable problem and the only way to solve it is to stop spending money you don't have. You will not be able to do that if you continue to junk-spend.

Remember: junk-spending is spending on anything that you don't actually need and which does not give you any genuine pleasure. Millions of people in debt have the same addiction to over-spending on junk. My method will cure this addiction; then you can begin the process of getting out of debt.

CREATING A VOID

The shock of birth leaves us desperately craving security. We reach for our mothers and they protect us. Our neediness and vulnerability continues through childhood, when we're cocooned from the harsh realities of life in a fantasy world of make-believe.

But before long we discover that Father Christmas and fairies do not exist. We look more critically at our parents, up until now our main towers of strength, and it begins to dawn on us that they are not the unshakeable pillars of strength that we had always imagined. They have weaknesses, frailties and fears just as we do.

The disillusionment leaves a void in our lives, which we tend to fill with pop stars, film stars, TV celebrities or sports personalities. We create our own fantasies. We make gods of these people and start to attribute to them qualities far in excess of those that they possess. We try to bask in their reflected glory. Instead of becoming complete, strong, secure and unique individuals in our own right, we become mere vassals, impressionable fans, leaving ourselves wide open to suggestion.

At the same time we're forced from the safety of home, to school and a new set of fears and insecurities. In the face of all this bewilderment and instability, we look for support, for a little boost now and then. We instinctively look to our role models and, quite naturally, copy the things they appear to be doing for comfort and relaxation: drink, smoke, shop.

THE FLAW IN THE INCREDIBLE MACHINE

The instinct to copy role models applies throughout the animal kingdom. 'Do as I do' is how the young learn to survive. So why, when it comes to humans, do we set examples to our young that threaten their very wellbeing. After all, is not man the greatest survivor of them all?

Compared to most animals, man is indeed an incredibly sophisticated machine. But there is a flaw in the machine, and the flaw can be traced to the very same thing that sets man above the rest of the animal kingdom: intellect.

Actually, it's not intellect itself that is the flaw, it's the way we apply it. Our intellectual ability to communicate and absorb information is quite incredible. It has given us music, art, literature, sport and science – things that set us apart from all other creatures on Earth. Unfortunately, we are also able to communicate and absorb misinformation. Our intellect can easily be fooled.

Take a look at this jumble of shapes. What does it say to you?

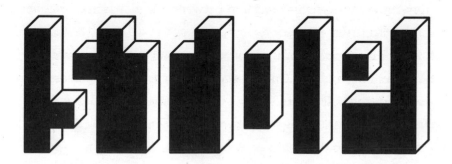

Is there a coherent message in it all? At first glance, it can look like a random line of building blocks. But there isn't really a meaningful message there at all, is there?

Now look again. This time, look at the shapes with your eyes half-closed and, by peering through your eyelashes, you can make a word appear. It might help if you move your head back a little (or to the side) and look at it from a distance.

Remember, you're not looking at the black type, you're looking at the white space between the type.

You should see the word STOP. Have you got it now? Obvious, isn't it? In fact, now that you can see it, I defy you to look at the same diagram and *not* see the word STOP. Now that you can see the pattern in the image, the truth will stay with you forever.

So why was it so hard to see in the first place? Because we're intellectually programmed to look for information in the black type on a white page, and the thought of doing the opposite doesn't cross our mind. The enticing words lead us further from the truth. We sense a connection between the words and look for an intellectual solution.

This is a graphic example of how easy it is to fool our intellect. Another example is an anaesthetic. Say you have a toothache; you reach for the painkillers. After a while the pain subsides and you feel better. But has the problem with your tooth gone away? Of course not. The pain has just been suppressed. And the pain was serving a useful purpose, it was telling your brain and body that there's a problem with your teeth, which needs sorting out.

By suppressing the pain and dealing with the symptom rather

than the cause, you prevent your body from responding to the problem appropriately and the most powerful healing agent is the body itself.

Imagine you're driving a car and the oil light comes on. What do you do? Remove the bulb from the warning indicator? Or pull over and top up the oil?

Both actions will stop the oil light from flashing; only one will prevent the engine from seizing up.

By using our intellect we have dispensed with the need to hunt for food, to gather fuel, to make fire and to avoid many dangers. Shops, power stations, cookers and the law take care of most of that for us. A consequence of this is that we tend to scorn our instincts in favour of our intellect. But our intellect has also created much greater horrors than any purely instinctive creature could ever devise.

HOW WE GET TRAPPED IN DEBT

Before we incur our first debt, we're aware of the arguments against it. We know that being in the red means paying money for nothing in the form of interest. We also know that debts can mount up if they're not properly managed. We might even be aware of the dire straits that some people get into, the repossessions, the marriage break-ups, the suicides. Intellectually we know that debt is something to be avoided.

However, we also know that millions of people live their lives in debt and seem to manage somehow. Meanwhile, Big Retail bombards us with inducements to spend money we don't have.

BUY THIS AFTERSHAVE!

WEAR THIS DRESS!

DRIVE THIS CAR!

TAKE THIS HOLIDAY!

These messages are accompanied by images of smiling, happy, beautiful people – just like us. Or rather, just like we would like to be. There's a void to fill and these enticements look like just the thing.

At the same time the credit companies start to circle like sharks. We've come to regard credit cards as status symbols, the trappings of being grown-up. What kid looking for a bit of respect wouldn't want to buy into that?

And so we take the plunge. The first debt is incurred and, joy of joys, we find it's not the end of the world. We can handle the repayments and we had some fun into the bargain. But the fun soon wears off and we're left looking for our next fix to fill the void. Now we feel more confident to take a debt on, and we push it a bit further. Rather than paying off that first debt and regaining control, we've used it as an argument to take on a bigger one. We're already losing control.

At first we're able to con ourselves that we remain in charge of our financial affairs and that there will be no problems. However, as time goes on and our difficulties increase, we begin to sense that we're slipping further and further into a bottomless pit. It's an unpleasant, insecure feeling that creates further anxiety and stress. Just as we reach for the painkillers to numb an aching tooth, we reach for a temporary fix to take away the unpleasant feeling caused by the debt: we go spending again. We use 'retail therapy' as our anaesthetic, rather than dealing with the real problem.

However, like any anaesthetic, it only lasts a short time. When it wears off, the stress is worse than before because we're further in debt. We now feel the need for another lift and turn to spending again. As time passes, we sense that the retail therapy is not working as effectively as it seemed to before and the tendency is to increase our spending to try to compensate. In this way we end up spending more and more and descending deeper and deeper into debt.

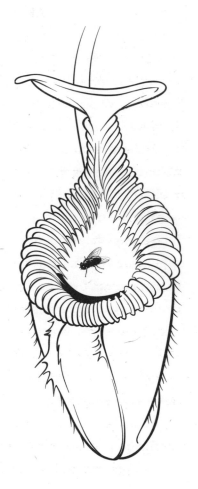

This is how the trap works. It's how any addiction works. The addict seeks relief in the very thing that's causing the misery. The trap is similar to a pitcher plant (*right*), which lures flies into its chamber with the sweet smell of nectar. The fly lands on the rim and begins to drink. The nectar tastes good; it seems like the best thing in the world. But it is the very thing that is luring the fly to its death.

The sides of the chamber are slippery and the fly is slowly sliding down towards the bottom where it will be digested. The fly senses something is wrong but that nectar has to be a good thing, doesn't it? And anyway, it can fly away any time it likes, can't it? Unfortunately not! By the time the fly realises the seriousness of the situation, its wings are stuck in the sticky nectar and it slides inexorably to its death. The pitcher plant claims another victim.

Like the fly, you only realise you're trapped in debt when you're well and truly stuck. The difference between the pitcher plant and the debt trap is that **IT IS NEVER TOO LATE TO ESCAPE FROM DEBT**.

You are not standing on a slippery slope; there is no physical force compelling you further into debt. The trap is entirely in your mind. The fact that you are your own jailer is an ingenious aspect of the trap but fortunately for you it's also its fatal weakness. You have the power to escape by understanding the nature of the trap and following the simple instructions in this book.

THE MYTH OF PLEASURE

We talk about 'retail therapy' but what do we actually mean?

You probably have good memories of certain shopping sprees, when you went out with a friend and blew some money on a few treats for yourself. But where did the real pleasure come from that day? Was it the queuing at various shop counters, waiting for your turn to pay? Was it the moment when you put your card into the card reader and punched in your PIN? Or when the cashier handed you your receipt? Was it really the spending that made your day? Or was it the company of your friend, the laughs you had together, the sheer pleasure of spending time with someone you're fond of?

The dream day that I described in Chapter 2 was not a dream because of the money I spent. The pleasure came from spending time and doing things with people whose company I enjoy.

I want you to understand that the whole concept of retail therapy is nonsense. It's the myth that Big Retail thrives on: the illusion that spending can alleviate our unpleasant feelings of emptiness, disillusionment and insecurity.

BUT IF THE BRAIN CAN BE DECEIVED INTO BELIEVING THAT SPENDING MAKES US HAPPY, DOES IT MATTER THAT IT ISN'T TRUE?

Of course it does, because the reality is that it's doing the complete opposite. It is forcing you deeper and deeper into debt and making you more and more miserable. Look at the STOP diagram. Once you see the truth as it really is, you'll never be fooled again.

THE TUG OF WAR OF FEAR

To unravel the brainwashing and reverse the process that has kept you in debt, we must first address your FEARS.

Addicts who attend our clinics arrive riddled with contradictions:

'Smoking is killing me but I can't handle stress without it.'

'I hate being overweight but I can't resist eating junk food.'

'I'd save a fortune if I quit the booze but I'd never enjoy a social occasion again.'

'I hate being controlled by drugs but I don't think I could cope without them.'

People with debt problems suffer the same confused emotions. You want to be free from debt but you're afraid that you won't be able to manage without it. This tug of war of fear is common to all addicts. You know that life in debt is a nightmare, but you're afraid that escaping from debt will be even worse. You want to change but at the same time you're frightened. Part of you has come to regard debt as your saviour, your safety belt, the only thing that has kept you afloat, and so you fear life without it. Get it clearly into your mind, debt has never been the solution, it has always been the problem.

When you escape from the trap you will discover that life becomes infinitely easier and more enjoyable than it is now and your only regret will be that you didn't set yourself free ages ago.

Yet right now you probably still find that hard to believe. That's OK, I don't expect you to understand everything until I've explained it all. And I will. For now, all I ask is that you keep an open mind. Question everything you read. If you don't understand it, go back and read it again. Open your mind to the reality of the situation. Confront your fears and realise that they are baseless.

The tug of war of fear shows that addicts recognise the rational advantages of quitting; the problem is that their mind is clouded by irrational fears. If you could focus only on the advantages and disregard the fears, you would find it easy to escape from the trap you're in.

Well, here's the good news: you can.

Those fears are merely illusions created by the massive amount of misinformation that we're fed from the day we're born. It's time to start reprogramming your intellect, in the same way that it was reprogrammed to see the STOP diagram. That means questioning the misconceptions that you have, until now, accepted as fact and opening your mind to the truth.

SUMMARY

- **Junk-spending is an addiction.**
- **Addictions are sustained by misplaced fears and delusions.**
- **The illusion of pleasure is a result of the brainwashing.**
- **Trust your instincts over your intellect.**
- **Addicts seek relief in the very thing that's causing the problem.**
- **Once you see the truth, you'll never be fooled again.**
- **Rejoice! You are on the road to solving your problem.**

Chapter 5

ILLUSIONS

IN THIS CHAPTER
• *BUYING AND SELLING MISINFORMATION* • *MIXED MESSAGES*
• *HOW WE FALL FOR CREDIT CARDS*
• *THE ILLUSION OF PLEASURE* • *WASTE*

Don't believe misinformation created to exploit you.

From birth our view of life is shaped by the influences surrounding us. Some of these influences are helpful, some not so helpful, and some extremely unhelpful. Our parents teach us to avoid dangers such as playing with fire or crossing the road without looking; our teachers show us what they want us to learn; the media show us the events they want us to see. In most cases these people are acting in good faith, doing their best to provide us with knowledge that will help us to lead safe, informed and fulfilling lives.

They all apply their own subjective slant to the views they expound, which are themselves influenced by their own parents, teachers and the media. This is the great advantage that mankind has over the rest of the animal kingdom: the ability to communicate knowledge through language and pictures. It means a wise man today can pass his knowledge on to someone 10 generations down the line, which allows every generation to build on the knowledge of its predecessors, enabling our species to develop way beyond the sophistication of other animals. But it also means that certain misconceptions can very quickly become accepted as fact.

THE COLD CALL

Now here's a fact that shouldn't surprise you.

THE WORLD IS FULL OF PEOPLE WITH A VESTED INTEREST IN SELLING YOU MISINFORMATION

Do you ever answer the phone at home around 6pm? If so, you'll recognise this conversation:

> YOU: *Hello*
>
> CALLER: *Hello, may I speak with* [your name, probably mispronounced]?
>
> YOU: *Speaking.*
>
> CALLER: *Good evening* [your name, mispronounced again]. *This is not a sales call…*

Ten seconds in and they've already told their first lie. You put the phone down. Or maybe you're too polite for that and you hear them out, or let them down gently. Whatever you do, as soon as you put the phone down they'll be calling someone else with the same lie.

We all know that anyone who cold calls you is trying to sell you something. They'll probably try to sweet talk you into giving your address so they can send you some information, or get you to commit to an appointment with one of their sales team. These are all just steps on the ladder to making a sale. And you can guarantee that the thing they're selling is something you don't need.

If it were something you needed, surely they'd just come out and offer it. 'Hello, madam. I'm selling household cleaning products door to door in your local area. Are you running low? I could save you a trip to the shops and they're cheaper than in the supermarket.'

Now that's what I call a sales proposition. But I've never received a cold call like that. Rather than come straight out with the proposition, the telesales person leads you in a complex game, like a fly fisherman playing a trout, luring you to the bait and avoiding the real proposition until they've got you well and truly on the hook.

Salespeople have many strategies for hooking their prey. These are well known among the sales fraternity. They have techniques for setting up a deal, techniques for closing one, techniques for re-opening negotiations that have broken down, techniques for getting those who have already bought to buy again... the list goes on, all of it preying on the weaknesses in human psychology.

One of the golden rules of selling is to fix an appointment, rather than trying to clinch the deal over the phone. Why? Because when people are face to face they find it harder to say no.

What does all this say to you? If they have to go to such lengths to manoeuvre us into a position where we feel obliged to buy, doesn't that suggest that we don't really want what they're selling?

I've used the example of telesales because it's widely

recognised as one of the most annoying examples of selling. The same techniques are applied everywhere in the commercial world: on television, in magazines, in the shops and online.

Advertising is about selling illusions. A beautiful, naked woman in a bath eats a chocolate bar as the water flows into the bubbles. You may have seen the ad. What adjectives spring to mind?

Beautiful

Sexual

Carefree

Luxurious

Naughty

But what other terms do we associate with chocolate, especially when excessive amounts are eaten?

Messy – it melts at body temperature and is almost impossible to eat without getting it all over your hands, mouth and clothes. In fact, a bath could be the safest place to eat it.

Unhealthy – too much chocolate rots your teeth, makes you fat and contains few healthy nutrients.

Unfulfilling – it won't leave you satisfied and once the initial sugar rush wears off you'll be left feeling emptier than before.

Advertisers know all this, so rather than telling us about the product, they create an image that distracts us from reality. We absorb the image and project it on to the product next time we see it for sale. That's how advertising works. Manufacturers spend a fortune creating and buying space for advertisements because our decisions to buy are so influenced by the images presented to us.

Advertisers and salespeople will argue that they are merely trying to persuade you to buy one brand over another, but actually they spend most of their time persuading people to buy products they don't need.

BUY ONE, GET ONE FREE

Another key to any sales strategy is creating the impression that they're not desperate for your money. They don't talk about selling, they talk about 'building a relationship'. In fact, they're so keen to build a relationship with you that they're going to put money in your pocket.

A bakery brand wants you to build a relationship with its cakes so it advertises a 'Half Price Offer', or 'Buy One, Get One Free' (BOGOF), or '50% Extra Free'. You see them everywhere in the shops and they always look attractive. For anyone managing a shopping budget, the idea of cutting costs wherever possible is appealing. 'Half price? Wow! That's a good deal.' You didn't want a cake, but hey, it's only half price.

So you begin your relationship with the cake, without pausing to weigh up whether 'half price' actually represents good value. There's a shop I know where the fruit is always half price. But who says it's half price? No one can remember what the full price was. To the passer-by who comes in for apples, that doesn't matter. They think their luck's in because they stumbled on a half-price offer.

'Buy One, Get One Free' is another sales trap. Remember that cake you didn't want? Well, now you can have two! That appeals to your sense of value.

So you buy two cakes that you don't want. You eat the first one but you leave it a while before eating the other one. By this time it's stale, so you throw it in the bin. 'What's the problem? I didn't pay for it in the first place. Easy come, easy go.'

Actually, you did pay for it. You may have only paid the price of one cake but that was money you weren't planning to spend. **EVEN AT HALF THE ADVERTISED PRICE, MONEY SPENT ON SOMETHING YOU DON'T WANT IS MONEY WASTED. IT'S ANOTHER CASE OF JUNK-SPENDING.**

For the baker, it's job done. For the price of the ingredients, he's got another customer to begin a relationship with his cake. You've sampled his product, and sampling is one of the most powerful persuaders for any sale. Before you fell for the sales trap you never had any intention of trying his cake. Now he knows there's a good chance you'll be back for more.

Does this remind you of the STOP diagram in the last chapter? At first glance you saw only enticing shapes. But once you stood back and saw the word STOP, you could never again be fooled into not seeing it. Now that you know the true message in the 'Half Price' and 'BOGOF' offers – i.e. buy something you don't want and get hooked – you'll see it every time.

GIVE THEM ENOUGH ROPE

There are many other sales traps that you need to see through, all of which are designed to entice you into buying something against your instincts. You're familiar with phrases such as:

Interest free credit

0% finance

Buy now, pay later

The language is carefully chosen to give the impression that they're not desperate for your money, they just want to help you. Don't be fooled. STOP. Listen to your instincts. If you weren't being offered 0% finance on the product in question, would you buy it? Or would you decide that you can't afford it?

If you feel you can't afford something, it's usually a sign that you don't really need or want it. When you really need or want something, you'll work hard and save your money so you can afford it. And this is what we tend to do as youngsters. Our natural instinct is not to spend money we don't have. However, in adulthood the money-lending companies give us the rope to hang ourselves and we become lazy and buy things we don't really need or want.

Perhaps you think I'm advocating harsh austerity. Not at all. Remember, my number one objective is your happiness. Chronic debt is caused by spending more money than you have. 'I can't afford it' is your instinct's way of protecting you from debt. The money-lenders are aware of this. That's why they devise so many tricks that say, 'Yes you can.'

Remember, money-lenders make their profit from debt. They want you to go into the red so they can hit you with extortionate interest rates. They want you to miss payments so that they can impose additional charges. Interest-free credit is their equivalent of the two-for-one cake; the ground-bait the angler throws into the water to lure the fish towards the hook; a throwaway offer of negligible value, designed to land the prize catch.

A MORE SINISTER ANALOGY IS THE DRUG PUSHER WHO HANDS OUT HEROIN TO SCHOOL CHILDREN, THEN PROFITS FROM THEM WHEN THEY GET HOOKED

IN HER OWN WORDS: JENNY

I had been struggling financially for some time but I expected to be promoted at work and receive a higher salary. On the strength of this assumption I went on a winter holiday with some girlfriends. Barbados was blissful and the hotel was fantastic. I found lots of things to buy for my flat and the jewellery was relatively cheap, especially the pearls. These would work nicely with the outfits I planned to get in the sales to complete my look in my new executive position. When I returned to London I swept through the last days of the sales, picking up everything at a discount. I was ready for my new life and I also looked forward, finally at 30, to being able to pay off my student loan.

I returned to work after the New Year and found they had appointed someone from outside the company to take the job I had expected. Shocked, disappointed and angry, I rashly resigned from the company where I had worked since finishing university.

There was a recession and, despite my qualifications and experience, it took me 18 months to find a new job. The new job paid a lower salary and was less satisfying than my previous one. By then I was in debt.

The offer from my credit card company to take a loan of £10,000 for six months at 0% seemed the answer to my problems. I took the money and paid off the card I had used for my holiday and shopping spree and the overdue bills that had accumulated and been put off by begging phone calls. The new funds arrived just in time as my mortgage holiday was due to end the following month. The hole in my pocket had got larger and larger. Now at least I could breathe again.

Five months later I received a letter from the credit card company reminding me that my interest was going to increase from the next statement. I wished I had the money to pay it off.

Jenny hoped she could pay off her debt. The credit card company hoped she couldn't.

When you go through your mail and it's a combination of overdue bills and seemingly attractive offers of 0% interest on your credit card, don't be tempted to sell your soul to the devil.

The credit card companies advertise 0% interest as a way of drawing you into borrowing, in the knowledge that you almost certainly won't be able to pay off your balance before the end of these beneficial terms and will spend perhaps the rest of your life paying interest more in the region of 20%.

HOLDING ALL THE CARDS

One of the most powerful illusions surrounds the credit card. The name, for a start, is inappropriate. Credit is a positive word: it means a commendation or approval, a source of honour, belief, trust, a good name. It is a figure in the plus column on a balance sheet. A more honest name would be 'debt card' or 'loan card'.

Calling it a credit card is the first step in creating the illusion that it is somehow a good thing to 'own'. Let's be quite clear: you don't own your credit card, it owns you and it can cast a sinister shadow over your everyday life.

But a credit card can take on an almost mystical power. It is seen as the key to all sorts of pleasures, an all-knowing fixer that opens doors, removes obstacles, solves problems and saves embarrassment. Of equal importance to what it can do for you is what it seems to say about you. A credit card is seen as a status symbol, something that can earn you respect.

We all want respect, especially when we're young, and the first offer of a credit card seems immensely flattering. What it appears to say is, 'We've done our homework and we regard you as somebody of substance, responsibility and maturity, who we can trust with thousands of pounds of our money.'

In fact, the wording they use isn't dissimilar to that. Who wouldn't be flattered by such an approach? Of course, what they're really saying is, 'We regard you as a potential victim, who will be glad of our offer of a loan, will spend freely on things you can't afford, are unlikely to pay off your balance at the end of each month and so will run up huge sums in interest.'

The card itself is designed to massage your ego further, stylishly crafted to look the part as an accessory that you would be proud to wave around in any trendy location. If you're very special, they might even give you a gold one.

The mystique is built up, layer upon layer, so that you come to regard your credit card as something that defines you. With it, you are all powerful; without it, you are nothing. The world has fallen for this illusion hook, line and sinker. It doesn't help that some businesses such as car hire firms ask for a credit card as security, as if anyone who doesn't have a credit card is less trustworthy. In fact, you can hire a car without a credit card, as I'll explain later.

The credit card has thus come to be regarded as an essential tool for anyone operating in the adult world.

STOP. Ignore the enticing words and the seductive images. See it for what it is. That piece of plastic is not your key to the world's treasures, it's the lender's key to yours. In signing up for your credit card, you give the lender control over your finances. Whereas you used to set the limit for what you spend, now they do. They hold all the cards – literally.

Banks make an obscene amount of money from the extortionate rates of interest they charge on credit cards and the tragedy is that they're taking the money from those who can least afford it. They start you off on a low limit to give you the confidence that they're looking after your interests, making sure you don't get into difficulties. They let you paddle around in the shallows for a while, then they allow you to go a little deeper. The water's lovely, everything's under control, you're a grown-up and you know what you're doing. You go deeper still, and suddenly you realise you're out of your depth. You keep paddling, faster now, using all your energy to keep your head above water, and somewhere in the back of your mind is the gnawing feeling that you're being circled by sharks.

Once you can see through all the hype and understand the truth about credit cards, they instantly lose their appeal. It's a bit like a science fiction movie where an enchanted object suddenly loses its special powers.

CAVEAT EMPTOR

If you want further proof that Big Retail relies on illusions, look no further than the salesperson's motto: *caveat emptor* – let the buyer beware. This is the legal principle that a buyer makes a purchase at his or her own risk and, therefore, the onus is on the buyer to carry out a thorough examination of the product before purchasing.

Would there be a need for such a principle if sellers were open and honest about all aspects of their product, good and bad? Of course not. *Caveat emptor* acknowledges that sellers tend to present the good points and omit the bad points, thereby creating an illusion.

We tend to regard this as fair play in our commerce-driven world. But what would happen if *caveat emptor* didn't apply, and sellers were obliged to point out all the bad points of their products? Any salesperson will tell you that they would sell a good deal less because customers would see the products for what they really are and realise that they neither need nor want them. The illusion would be stripped away.

In fact, a huge amount of spending is the result of an illusion: the illusion that it will make us happy.

THE ILLUSION OF PLEASURE

A little boy is alone in his room. He feels lonely so he calls to his father. He wants his dad to play with him but dad is busy. His father feels for his son and wants him to be happy, so he goes out and buys him a toy – something the child has seen on television and has expressed an interest in. At first the child is delighted to receive the toy, but when he gets it out of the box he finds it's not as exciting as it was made to look on TV. He tries to play with it for a while but it bores him. What he really wants isn't colourful plastic but companionship and love. He throws the toy against the wall and smashes it. His father hears the noise and comes running. He's angry. The little boy cries. His father feels awkward and wants to cheer him up. He goes out and buys another toy – a bigger, more expensive one. He gives it to his son, then leaves him to play on his own.

Once again, the initial flush of excitement soon wears off and the pattern repeats itself. Over time, the boy develops a lifestyle in which the only highs are the moments when his father gives him a new toy. He becomes dependent on those gifts, even though they offer no lasting pleasure. Occasionally he will expect a toy and his dad will not come up with the goods. Then all hell breaks out. The boy shouts and screams at his father, who only knows one way to placate him. So the pattern for a sad and unfulfilling life is set.

We can all see the flaws in this scenario. It's obvious that the father's mistake is trying to please his son by buying him toys, when what he really wants are things that cost nothing but are worth the world: attention, affection, companionship, love.

WHY CAN'T WE SEE THAT IN OUR OWN LIVES?

If you charted the emotional wellbeing of the spoilt child on a graph, it would look the same as the graph for an addict, like this:

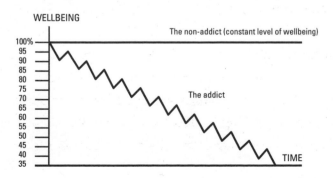

If we say our level of happiness before the pattern starts is 100, you can see how it falls as the pattern persists. Whatever it is that initially makes us unhappy (the little boy's loneliness, for example) takes our level down to 90. We spend some money on ourselves and experience a temporary boost, taking our level up to 95. But as the fix wears off and we feel guilty and stupid that we've just dug ourselves deeper into debt, the void deepens and we feel more unhappy than before. Our level sinks to 85. The next fix kicks it up to 90, but it soon falls again to 80 as the misery of being in debt increasingly takes its toll.

And so it goes on. You never quite return to the level of happiness you started with because as you go deeper and deeper into debt the effects on your wellbeing and quality of life become increasingly severe. The short-lived boosts create the illusion of pleasure, but the reality is a steady decline into abject misery.

SEEING IT FOR REAL

The idea that money buys happiness is a myth. You can see it plainly in the case of the spoilt child, now you need to see it in your own case. The reality of spending money you haven't got is far from happy.

OVER-SPENDING LEADS TO:

Being a slave to debt

Fear

Evasiveness

Stress

Loss of trust and respect

Breakdown of relationships

Legal problems

Misery

It is also responsible for waste and pollution on a global scale that is destroying the planet and our own health. Further evidence that money does not buy happiness is seen in the amount we throw away. Many of the things we buy end up in the bin. The average waste per head in the developed world is around one ton per year. Imagine emptying that much outside your house in one go.

Of course it doesn't pile up outside your house, it gets buried in the ground, in landfill sites so vast they can be seen from space, or it gets washed out to sea, where it gathers in gyroscopic currents in the middle of our oceans, killing fish and polluting the water.

Next time you feel tempted to go out and buy some happiness, think of those landfill sites and ask yourself how long it will be before your new purchases are festering among them?

SUMMARY

- Watch out for people with a vested interest in selling you misinformation.
- Don't buy the illusions on offer.
- If your instinct tells you 'I can't afford it,' listen!
- Happiness is the sign of success, not money.
- A credit card hands control of your finances to the lender.
- The illusion of pleasure keeps us in the trap.

Chapter 6

FEAR

IN THIS CHAPTER
• *FEAR OF FAILURE* • *FEAR OF SUCCESS*
• *THE MYTH OF SACRIFICE*
• *ALL YOU HAVE TO GAIN*

The fear that keeps people in debt is based solely on illusions.

When you're in debt you're trapped in a prison. Every aspect of your life is controlled by your debts: your daily routine, your hopes, your view of the world, your suffering. Of course, you're not physically imprisoned. There are no walls or bars. The prison is in your mind. However, as long as you remain a slave to debt, you will experience the same psychological symptoms as an inmate in a physical prison.

It's a sad fact of the penal system that many long-term prisoners start re-offending soon after they are released. This depressing phenomenon occurs not just because they haven't learnt the error of their ways, but because in some cases they actually *want* to go back inside. They yearn for the 'security' of the prison. Life on the outside is alien and frightening for them once they are 'institutionalized', far more frightening than life on the inside. It's not what they know. They don't feel equipped to handle it.

The same fear afflicts drug addicts. They're afraid that they won't be able to enjoy or cope with life without their drug, that they'll have to go through some terrible trauma to come off it and that they'll be condemned to a life of sacrifice and deprivation. And what if they fail?

THE FEAR OF FAILURE

The fear of failure is one of the excuses used by addicts as a reason for not trying to get free. This fear is illogical. It is the fear of something that has already happened.

The failure is the fact that they are an addict. As long as they remain an addict, they will remain a failure.

The same thing applies to debt: **YOU NOW OWE MONEY AND IT'S MAKING YOUR LIFE A MISERY. AS LONG AS THAT CONTINUES, YOU WILL CONTINUE TO FEEL A FAILURE.**

When channelled properly, the fear of failure can be a positive force. It's the emotion that focuses the mind of the runner at the starting blocks, the ballerina waiting in the wings and the student going into an exam.

Fear of failure is the little voice in your head that reminds you to prepare thoroughly, to remember everything you've rehearsed and trained for and to leave nothing to chance. It's what drives people on to achieve.

But the obstacle that stands in the way of you now is, in fact, the fear of success. That may sound like a contradiction. Why should anyone fear success? Isn't that what we all strive for?

SUCCESS v FAILURE

In the case of the person suffering from debt, failure means remaining in the old, familiar prison cell; success means coming out into the unknown and that can seem daunting. Like those long-term prisoners, you may be fearful of what life will be like outside and dread the self-discipline, sacrifice and deprivation that you fear will be inevitable.

Perhaps you've been tricked into believing that being debt-free is boring. Though you're well aware of the misery that being in debt causes, you may now have come to think of it as part of your identity. Perhaps you even regard it with a perverse kind of respect, as if there were some sort of shambolic charisma about it. The image of the chain smoker, the heavy drinker and the spendthrift can suggest that it makes us an interesting character.

It's not hard to understand why. The heroic characters in books and films are frequently portrayed as having one or more of these characteristics and the implication is that it makes them human, charming, exciting and interesting. To the audience maybe – in real life it makes them miserable.

Cast the illusions aside and be clear in your mind: the panic feeling that makes you afraid to even try to get out of debt is caused by junk-spending, not relieved by it. And one of the greatest benefits you'll receive when you quit is never to suffer it again.

If I could transport you into the future and show you how you will feel when you finish this book, you would think, 'Will I really feel this good?' Fear will have been replaced by elation, despair by optimism, self-doubt by confidence, apathy by dynamism. As a result of these psychological turnarounds, your physical health will improve too. You will enjoy a newfound energy, as well as the ability to truly relax.

THE SIMPLE FACT IS THIS: TAKE AWAY THE JUNK-SPENDING AND THE FEAR GOES TOO

Maybe you've tried to stop junk-spending in the past and gone for weeks, months, even years, but still found that you missed it. Trust me, this method is different. You will not miss it. You are not giving anything up. There is no sacrifice involved. Instead, you are removing something from your life that has made you miserable and are replacing it with something that makes you genuinely happy. You are trading lack of control over your spending for total control; no choice for absolute choice.

Like the cigarette for the smoker and the bottle for the drinker, part of you feels that debt is your friend, your constant companion and crutch. Get it clearly into your mind, this is an illusion. In reality it's your worst enemy and, far from supporting you, it's driving you deeper and deeper into misery. You instinctively know this. So open your mind and follow your instincts.

EVERYTHING TO GAIN

Think about all the good things you stand to gain by getting out of debt. Think of the enormous self-respect you'll regain, the time and energy you'll save by not having to keep dodging your creditors, the pleasure of re-establishing friendships free from the complications of debt, and the absence of fear and panic whenever you hear a letter land on the mat or you check your bank balance.

So far I have given you three instructions to put you in the right frame of mind so that this book can help you get out of debt.

1. Follow all the instructions
2. Keep an open mind
3. Begin with a feeling of elation.

If you are struggling with any of these instructions, go back and re-read the relevant chapters.

We have established that your debt problem does absolutely nothing positive for you whatsoever, that the beliefs that have trapped you in debt are merely illusions, and that you have everything to gain and nothing to lose by getting out of debt.

That process involves some simple changes to the way you handle your money, changes that, up until now, you have been afraid to make.

BUT NOW WE ARE AGREED THAT THERE IS NOTHING TO FEAR. LIFE WILL BECOME INFINITELY MORE ENJOYABLE FROM THE MOMENT YOU BEGIN THE PROCESS.

Perhaps you're afraid that the process itself will be painful. You may have struggled to get out of debt before by using willpower and found it a nightmare. That's because the willpower method doesn't work. It leaves you feeling deprived and so, as I will explain in the next chapter, you never really get completely free.

SUMMARY

- Over-spending doesn't relieve the fear and panic, it makes it much worse.

- You are not giving anything up.

- Open your mind to the marvellous gains of finally ending your debt problem.

- Remove the misconceptions and you remove the fear.

Chapter 7

WILLPOWER

IN THIS CHAPTER

- *TAKING THE DIFFICULT OPTION* • *DO YOU THINK YOU'RE WEAK-WILLED?*
- *A NEVER-ENDING STRUGGLE* • *CROSSING THE LINE THE EASY WAY*
- *OTHER QUITTERS*

If you think you have failed to solve your debt problems before now because you lack the willpower, think again. With this method you don't need willpower.

PUSH OPEN THE DOOR

If it's so easy to get out of debt, why do so many people find it incredibly hard? The reason is simple: they're going about it the wrong way.

The simplest of tasks becomes difficult if you use the wrong method. Crossing the road, for example, is easy if you go about it sensibly. But try doing it with your eyes closed, drunk, in heavy traffic, and you make something which is easy into a virtual impossibility by going about it in the wrong way.

Most over-spenders find it difficult to stop because they use the willpower method. They have a constant conflict of will, a mental tug-of-war. On one side, your rational mind knows you should stop over-spending because it's costing you a fortune, controlling your life and causing you misery. On the other hand, your addicted brain makes you panic at the thought of being deprived of your pleasure or crutch. With the willpower method, you focus on all the reasons for stopping and hope you can last for long enough without over-spending so that the desire to do so eventually goes.

The problem with this is that you still perceive over-spending as providing you with benefits, and therefore you feel you've made a sacrifice. Because you feel deprived, you become miserable, which in turn makes you want to cheer yourself up by doing the one thing you've vowed not to do – over-spend again.

You don't need willpower to stop if there's no conflict of will. We are going to resolve the conflict by removing doubt from your mind and making you see that over-spending provides you with no benefits whatsoever.

USING WILLPOWER FOR THE REST OF YOUR LIFE TO PREVENT YOU FROM OVER-SPENDING WILL NOT MAKE YOU HAPPY; REMOVING THE NEED AND DESIRE TO OVER-SPEND WILL

Some people do manage to quit smoking, drinking, over-eating, or over-spending through sheer force of will, but they never really get completely free from their problem, as I will explain in a moment. In most cases, the willpower method fails and you end up back in the trap, even more miserable than before.

DO YOU THINK YOU'RE WEAK-WILLED?

Because people think it takes willpower to change behaviour – whether it's smoking, drinking, over-eating or over-spending – those who fail to quit are generally branded as weak-willed. Perhaps you think that's why you've been unable to get out of debt up until now: because you lack the strength of will. If that's the case, then you haven't yet understood the nature of the trap you're in.

Ask yourself whether you're weak-willed in other ways. Perhaps you're a smoker or you eat or drink too much, and you regard these conditions as further evidence of a weak will. There is a connection between all addictions, but it isn't that they are signs of a lack of willpower. On the contrary, they are more likely evidence of a strong will. What they share is that they are all traps created by misleading information and untruths. And one of the most misleading untruths is that quitting requires willpower.

IN HIS OWN WORDS: CHARLES

I was a keen sportsman in my youth and I was on the brink of becoming an international hockey player when I suffered an injury that ended my career. It was devastating at the time, but I picked myself up and threw myself into a career in marketing.

I did well and made pretty good money, but by the time payday came round each month, I had always emptied my account. I liked to socialise and buy gifts for my girlfriend – and myself, if I'm honest. Almost without realising, I began spending more money each month than I earned, which meant I was slipping further and further into the red. After two years of this I had about £8,000 on my credit card, but I told myself that I could make the decision to 'tighten my belt' any time I chose and pay that off in three or four months. No problem.

That time came when I proposed to my girlfriend and she agreed to marry me. I knew we'd need money for the wedding and to buy a house, so I decided to cut back on my spending, pay off my debts and start saving. But I found I couldn't do it. I set myself a strict spending plan, but no matter how hard I tried, I just couldn't stick to it. I didn't have the willpower and I couldn't understand why. I had always been incredibly determined in sport, which was how I had reached such a high level, and it had also helped me progress in my career.

I didn't like to be beaten and I always thought I had the grit to withstand any challenge, but the more I tried, the harder I found it to stick to my spending plan and the more frustrated I became. For the first time in my life, I felt like a failure. I was constantly letting myself down, so I tried to cheer myself up by spending more.

I realise now what my problem was: I believed I was making a genuine sacrifice by cutting back on my spending and the more I willed myself to fight it, the bigger that sacrifice appeared to be.

It takes a strong-willed person to persist in doing something that goes against all their instincts.

You know your spending is dragging you deeper and deeper into debt, making you increasingly stressed and unhappy, threatening to destroy your relationships, your career and your life. Yet you continue to do it. That's not the behaviour of a weak-willed person.

Going on a shopping spree, even though you know you have no money to spend; charging an item that takes your fancy to your card, even though you know you're already failing to make the repayments on your current balance and will only put yourself under more pressure; stubbornly ignoring the advice of those around you and continuing to over-spend; all these are the actions of a strong-willed person.

> **IF I SAW YOU TRYING TO CROSS THE ROAD BLINDFOLD AND I TOLD YOU YOU'D FIND IT EASIER IF YOU ALLOWED YOURSELF TO SEE, BUT YOU IGNORED ME AND INSISTED ON TRYING TO CROSS BLINDFOLD, I'D CALL YOU STRONG-WILLED, NOT WEAK-WILLED**

The ex-con who re-offends soon after being released from prison is not weak-willed; he is showing a strong will to get back inside. It takes real determination to commit a crime.

Think of all the people you know who have had debt problems. It's probably a small list because nobody likes to admit to it. But there are enough high-profile examples to illustrate that severe debt is not a problem exclusive to the weak-willed.

Former US President Thomas Jefferson, for example, left office in 1809 owing $10,000 on wine alone. When he died, his estate and all his possessions were auctioned off to pay his creditors.

The field of entertainment offers many examples of super-rich stars who have fallen deeply into debt. Elvis Presley and Michael Jackson ran up enormous debts, despite the income from their phenomenal singing careers. Elton John admitted to running up debts of over £1.5 million a month, the result of a lavish lifestyle that included £290,000 spent on flowers in one year. Hollywood stars Mickey Rooney, Burt Reynolds and Kim Basinger all filed for bankruptcy in the 1990s, and boxer Mike Tyson, the former heavyweight champion of the world, followed suit in 2003.

Donald Trump found himself in $1.8 billion worth of debt in 2003 and British newspaper magnate Robert Maxwell, who drowned in a mysterious boating incident in 1991, took £440 million from his employees' pension fund to finance his enormous debts.

I offer these examples not to make you feel that your debts are minor in comparison, but to show that people in debt are not necessarily weak-willed.

YOU DON'T BECOME A GLOBAL SUPERSTAR, A BUSINESS TYCOON OR A US PRESIDENT IF YOU'RE WEAK-WILLED. YOU HAVE TO BE INCREDIBLY STRONG-WILLED

If you think about it, you can, I'm sure, find evidence that you too are strong-willed. For example, when your creditors start putting pressure on you, what lengths do you go to to avoid them? Do you cave in at the first ounce of pressure?

Or do you find any way you can to dodge clearing your debts? That takes willpower. In fact, the time and energy you put into staying in debt is phenomenal.

How do you react when people tell you that you should change your ways? Do you find that you tend to do the opposite? Wouldn't you describe that as wilful?

Ironically, very strong-willed people can have particular difficulty on the willpower method, because, like a strong-willed child, they keep their tantrum going for longer at a greater intensity, whereas a weaker-willed person gives up moping more quickly. Who screams longest and loudest in a tantrum, a strong-willed child or a weak-willed one?

IN HIS OWN WORDS: JOHN

I once went four months without spending on anything other than necessities. My only expenditure was paying the bills, repayments and interest on my loans, transport to and from work, and food. It took all my willpower to stick to my regime but my debts were starting to get under control and I really believed that I might be able to clear them after all, provided I stuck at it.

But then I caved in. I couldn't stand the strain any longer. I felt deprived at not being able to go out on the spending sprees that had got me into debt in the first place and, having been so good for months, I felt I deserved a reward. So I went out and blew a load of money on my credit card. I felt a sense of relief at having finally caved in and not having to deprive myself by using willpower any more, but rather than feeling happy, I broke down and cried because I had failed.

John had strained every sinew, gritted his teeth and dug in, determined not to over-spend again. But before he managed to clear his debts his willpower ran out.

He thought he was in range of the finishing line, the point at which he would become debt-free, and that was why he felt so miserable. If only he could have lasted a little longer.

In fact, John wasn't in range of the finishing line at all, he only thought he was. While he was still moping about not allowing himself to over-spend, he was never going to get free.

Let me be quite clear, this book is not just about becoming debt-free, although that's a crucial part of it, it's also about removing the desire to over-spend so that you never fall into the trap again.

The simple truth is that if you try to quit by using the willpower method, the struggle may never end. As long as you continue to suffer the illusion that you're making a sacrifice, you'll continue to feel deprived and you'll never be completely free.

SOLVING THE PROBLEM

With this method, the elation of crossing the finishing line comes as soon as you remove the fear and illusions and stop incurring new debts. That's when you become free from the mental prison and psychological torture that is currently making your life a misery. You need to understand that you'll only get to that line if you're in a positive frame of mind.

If you continue to believe that you have to suffer an indeterminate period of misery, you'll feel fearful, deprived and miserable, you'll again find yourself seeking to relieve those feelings by over-spending and you'll fall back into the trap.

Once you've failed with the willpower method, making another attempt is even more daunting because you've reinforced the illusion that it is very difficult, if not impossible, to solve your problem.

When you first give up on the willpower method by going on a spending spree, you do get a feeling of relief. It's important to understand that this is not a genuine pleasure but simply a temporary relief from self-inflicted suffering.

You had been feeling deprived because you were using willpower to fight the desire to over-spend. When you give in, you can finally stop using willpower at that moment and, of course, that's a relief. However, you only felt deprived because you were suffering the illusion that over-spending gave you a genuine pleasure or crutch. In reality it does neither and once you've given in, you're again tortured by feelings of failure and foreboding, guilt and disappointment.

YOU DON'T NEED WILLPOWER TO GET FREE

You only need willpower if there is a conflict of will going on inside your head, a tug of war in your mind. Take away one side of the tug of war and there is nothing to fight against. It's easy.

YOU DON'T HAVE TO WAIT UNTIL YOU'VE CLEARED ALL YOUR DEBTS TO BE HAPPY AND FREE FROM ANXIETY

On the contrary, once we've removed the brainwashing, the fears and the illusions, you can begin the process of getting out of debt with a feeling of elation.

OTHER QUITTERS

You may know people who are trying to get out of debt, or cure some other addiction, using willpower. You may admire them and wish you could do the same. STOP.

Remember what I have told you about the willpower method and see things as they really are.

People who try to quit by the willpower method can have a harmful effect on you.

They either talk proudly about the sacrifices they're making, or they moan about them. Either way, they reinforce the misconception that quitting demands sacrifice.

IT IS IMPORTANT THAT YOU IGNORE THE ADVICE OF ANYONE WHO CLAIMS TO HAVE QUIT BY THE WILLPOWER METHOD. THE BEAUTIFUL TRUTH IS THERE IS NO SACRIFICE

You are about to solve your over-spending problem. To do that, you need to understand that you are not giving anything up. You only need willpower if you are caught up in the tug of war of fear. Take away the fear and there is no conflict. It's easy.

You don't have to wait until you have paid off your debts before knowing that your problem is solved.

You succeed from the moment you unravel all the illusions that have kept you in the debt trap, free yourself from fear and begin the process of getting out of debt with a feeling of elation.

If you've followed all the instructions so far and understood that the perceptions that have kept you in the debt trap are illusions, that it doesn't take willpower to escape the trap, and that there is nothing to fear, you should already be feeling a sense of elation. You have taken a major step in solving your debt problems. You can start living your life again, knowing that you are no longer a slave to debt. You are in control and soon you will be debt-free.

ISN'T THAT SOMETHING WORTH CELEBRATING?

There is only one more obstacle that could be preventing you from feeling a sense of elation: the belief that you have an addictive personality, and so will never be able to stop over-spending or free yourself from the desire to over-spend.

Don't worry. In the next chapter I will explain why this is just another illusion.

SUMMARY

- Becoming free is only hard if you use the wrong method.
- Debt is not a symptom of being weak-willed. In fact, it's often the opposite.
- With the willpower method, you are never free.
- With Easyway, you are free the moment you reverse the brainwashing and stop incurring new debt.

Chapter 8

THE ADDICTIVE PERSONALITY

IN THIS CHAPTER
•A CONVENIENT EXCUSE •WHY SOME PEOPLE SEEM TO BE MORE
SUSCEPTIBLE THAN OTHERS •A DIFFERENT BREED
•THE EVIDENCE OF HISTORY •THE EFFECT, NOT THE CAUSE

The theory of the addictive personality stems from looking at the situation from the wrong perspective. The character traits shared by addicts are not the cause of their addiction, they are the outcome.

In the same way that addicts believe they lack the willpower to quit, many of them also believe that their problem is peculiar to them. People in debt are particularly good at making such excuses:

'I've been cleaned out by a divorce.'

'I'm in a low-paid job.'

'I have to maintain an affluent image in my line of work.'

'My parents weren't rich.'

'I'm plagued by bad luck.'

'I'm a generous person.'

Even when it's pointed out that their problem is an addiction to spending money they don't have, they're ready with the excuse:

'I have an addictive personality.'

Many addicts believe that there's something in their genetic or chemical make-up that makes it hard for them to quit. Sadly, this misconception is backed up by so-called experts who support the theory of the addictive personality. The term is bandied about so often that it's easy to be fooled into believing it's a recognised condition. It's not. It's a theory, largely based on the incidence of multiple addictions in the same person, e.g. alcoholics who are also smokers or gamblers, or heroin addicts who are heavily in debt.

All these addictions are caused by the same thing but it's not the personality, it's the misguided belief that the thing you are addicted to gives you a genuine pleasure or crutch.

REMEMBER, THE MISERY OF THE ADDICT IS NOT RELIEVED BY THE THING THEY ARE ADDICTED TO, IT'S CAUSED BY IT

The addictive personality theory gives addicts an excuse to avoid even trying to quit. If you think you have an addictive personality, you will regard quitting as an impossible task. 'How can I override my own genetic make-up?' This illusion can also be reinforced by your failed attempts to quit by using willpower.

It is further confirmed by the whingers, who have quit by using the willpower method and are feeling deprived because they still believe they're making a sacrifice. After all, if they have abstained for years and are still craving their little crutch, surely there must be some flaw in their genetic make-up that keeps drawing them back?

NO. THEY'RE DRAWN BACK BECAUSE THEY HAVE NOT UNDERSTOOD THE REALITY OF THE SITUATION AND ARE STILL LABOURING UNDER THE MISCONCEPTION THAT THEY HAVE MADE A SACRIFICE

Don't be fooled by these illusions. Pleading an addictive personality is just another cop-out. You don't want to stay trapped in debt, with all the fear, misery and hardship that goes with it, that's why you're reading this book. You have made the decision to escape and I am going to show you how. It's easy, provided you keep an open mind. If you cling to the excuse that you have an addictive personality, it means that your mind is not open and you risk sentencing yourself to remain in the prison for the rest of your life.

It may sound as if I'm accusing addicts of lying to themselves and their families. I'm not. The illusion is caused by the confusion of contradictory facts, misinformation, anomalies and general ignorance that is spread around so freely. I'm not belittling addicts. How could I? I have been in that trap myself, right up to my neck.

I don't regard myself as stupid. I know now that the spread of misinformation is so relentless that anybody can be conned, and most people are to some extent. But once you understand the true picture, the illusions disappear and you realise that you are complete without your addiction. With it, you are a slave.

DEGREES OF ADDICTION

So why do some people fall deeper into the trap than others? Why can someone have a puff of a cigarette and never touch one again, while another gets hooked and ends up smoking sixty a day? Doesn't that suggest that one has an addictive personality and the other doesn't?

It suggests a difference between them, certainly, but there are numerous differences between people which can explain why one person's behaviour differs from another person's in this context and none of them has anything to with an addictive personality.

Some people find the first puff so revolting that they don't have the willpower to go through the process of getting hooked. Some people's lungs cannot tolerate the poisoning. Some can't afford to smoke sixty a day.

Some find it impossible to find the time or space to smoke sixty a day, particularly since the bans on smoking in public places. In addition to that, our behaviour is intimately linked to the influences we are subjected to as we grow up: different parents, teachers, friends, the things we read, watch and listen to, the places we go, the people we meet, etc.

AN AFFINITY BETWEEN WEAKNESSES

Another factor that can make you think you have an addictive personality is that people with the same problem as you can seem to be a different breed from everyone else. This is reinforced by the fact that you appear to share similar character traits: an unstable temperament, which swings between exuberance and misery, a tendency towards excess, a high susceptibility to stress, evasiveness, anxiety and insecurity. The temptation is to believe that these character traits are evidence of the addictive personality that led you into debt.

Of course, the reality is that they are the *result* of being in debt.

The reason addicts feel more comfortable in the company of similar addicts is not because they're more interesting or fun; on the contrary, the attraction lies in the very fact that they won't challenge you or make you think twice about your addiction because they're in the same boat.

It feels as if there's safety in numbers. All addicts know that they're doing something profoundly stupid. If they're surrounded by other people doing the same thing, they don't feel quite so idiotic.

The good news is that, once you're free from the addiction, you also get free from the harmful effects it has on your character.

THE EVIDENCE OF HISTORY

If there were a gene that predisposed people to become addicts, you would expect the percentage of addicts in the world to have remained fairly constant throughout history. Yet this is not the case. Take smoking: in the 1940s over 80 per cent of the UK adult male population was hooked on nicotine; today it's under 25 per cent. A similar trend is evident throughout most of Western Europe and the United States. So are we to conclude that the proportion of people with addictive personalities has fallen by a whopping 55 per cent in just over half a century?

At the same time, the number of smokers in Asia has soared. What complex genetic anomaly is this that rises and falls so rapidly, and even appears to transfer itself wholesale from one continent to another?

EFFECT NOT CAUSE

The fact is you didn't get into debt because you have an addictive personality. If you think you have an addictive personality, it's simply because you got addicted to over-spending. This is the trick that addiction plays on you.

It makes you feel that you're dependent on your addiction and that there's some weakness in your character or genetic make-up. It distorts your perceptions and thereby maintains its grip on you.

ONCE THE ILLUSIONS HAVE BEEN STRIPPED AWAY AND YOU SEE THE SITUATION AS IT REALLY IS, YOU'LL WONDER HOW YOU WERE EVER CONNED INTO SEEING IT DIFFERENTLY AND YOU WILL BE FREE

The addictive personality theory promotes the belief that there's something wrong with the way you've been wired and that you are, therefore, condemned to a life of slavery and misery. I promise you, nothing could be further from the truth.

In fact, one of the greatest gains you will be making as a result of reading this book is to realise that the problem does not result from your character or personality and to be able to look forward to a bright future of freedom and happiness.

SUMMARY

• The addictive personality is a myth that gives the addict an excuse to avoid even trying to escape.

• The personality traits shared by addicts are caused by their addiction, they are not the cause of the addiction.

• Once you accept that an addictive personality is not to blame for your problem, then you can set about getting free.

Chapter 9

GETTING HOOKED

IN THIS CHAPTER
- *WHY DOESN'T EVERYONE HAVE DEBT PROBLEMS?*
- *RECOGNIZING YOUR POWER TO CHOOSE* • *NEED v WANT*
- *OUR REASONS FOR SPENDING* • *FILLING THE VOID* • *ANY EASY CHOICE*

The belief that we have no choice in certain areas of spending leaves us extremely vulnerable to the debt trap. Once we start to conform to what we think is an inevitable path, debt is only a short step away.

So if debt problems have nothing to do with an addictive personality or with your genetic make-up, why is it that some people get heavily into debt and others don't?

When I first devised my method, it focused exclusively on smoking but I always knew that it could be applied to alcoholism and other drug addictions. Although the drug may vary, the principle remains the same: the addict is deluded into believing the drug provides a genuine pleasure or crutch, when, in fact, it does the opposite.

When it came to over-eating, the similarity was not so clear. After all, unlike addictive drugs that destroy you, food is essential for our survival. The breakthrough came with the realization that the problem was not simply eating too much food, but eating the wrong kind of food. We refer to it as 'junk food', by which we don't mean only fast food, sweets, etc, but all foods that are altered from their natural state.

IT IS ESSENTIAL FOR MANKIND TO EAT FOOD, BUT NOT ALL SO-CALLED FOOD IS ESSENTIAL

In fact, much of the food we buy is non-essential. By that I mean it does virtually nothing for us in terms of vitamins, minerals and energy. In fact, it hardly qualifies as food at all. We buy it because there are huge, powerful marketing organizations out there that constantly tell us to, and con us into believing false information about the products they sell.

These junk foods are addictive. They contain high levels of refined sugar and salt, which we mistake for the natural sugars and minerals that our body needs. We become hooked on these 'drug foods' and find we can't stop eating them. Because they don't contain the nutrients we need, they never satisfy our true hunger, so we keep on eating. We find ourselves stuffed but still hungry. This is why such a huge proportion of the developed world is obese.

Understanding the over-eating problem helps us to understand the debt problem. Just as the problem with over-eating is not food, but the wrong type of food, the problem with debt is not spending, but the wrong type of spending.

It's what I call junk-spending.

ESSENTIAL DEBT

I mentioned earlier that just about everybody feels governed by money to some extent. They may have what they consider an unavoidable debt, for example a mortgage, a car loan or a student loan. These are debts they took on in order to acquire what they considered to be essentials: shelter, transport, education.

So is there such a thing as an essential debt? Is it not the case that in order to make your way in a developed society, you have to acquire certain properties or services, which, unless you are lucky enough to have vast personal wealth, can only be acquired by incurring some degree of debt?

The obvious answer is yes. The actual answer is no. Think about it: nobody *has* to own a car, nobody *has* to go to college and nobody *has* to own a house.

'Oh no, here we go! He's going to tell me I have to live in a shack and fetch water from a stream.'

Not so – although you could if you wanted to. Some people do choose such a way of life and are very happy with it. I am merely stating that none of these things are essential to our survival on this planet. They are all choices we make in the belief that they will enhance our quality of life. You may believe that with every purchase you have made, every debt you've incurred, money has gone on something that improves your quality of life. After all, why would anyone spend money if doing so makes them miserable?

And yet, in your case, it has. That's exactly why you've come to be reading this book.

Remember, my number one objective is your happiness. I want

you to enjoy life. In order to achieve that, it's important to accept that every debt you incur is a matter of personal choice. Although it may seem as if the society you live in forces you to take on debts in order to get by, in reality you are free to choose.

NEED v WANT

Once you're hooked on junk-spending, when you make a purchase, whether it's handing over your money at the counter, clicking 'buy now' online or giving your credit card details, you feel a slight buzz of exhilaration. It's fleeting, like the first hit of nicotine from a cigarette, and when it's gone it leaves an empty feeling, a come-down. But instead of realizing that spending causes the empty feeling, we're fooled into thinking it relieves it.

Therefore, when we feel empty, we seek to fill the void by creating the buzz of the transaction.

Next time you're about to buy something, try to identify your motivation. Be honest with yourself. There are a number of factors that play a part in much of our spending:

Boredom

Sadness

Stress

Routine

Reward

Envy

Apart from food, it's rare that we buy anything because we really need it. Not *want* it, *need* it. Want is a sensation caused by the things listed above. It is the desire to fill an emotional void. Need is fundamental to preserving your survival.

'So you're telling me I don't *need* a new pair of shoes because the old ones aren't killing me.'

Actually, no. Wearing old shoes that look shabby and feel worn out is a miserable experience. I don't want you to feel miserable. So if your old, worn-out shoes are making you miserable, I would argue that you do *need* a new pair.

Of course, the distinction between want and need varies from person to person, because need includes the need for happiness. The important thing is to be honest with yourself. The more you practise, stopping to think about want and need every time you spend, the better you will become at quickly identifying the purchases you don't need.

To begin with, try applying the golden rule put forward by William Morris, the 19th century English designer and thinker, most famous for his beautiful textile designs:

'Have nothing in your house that you do not know to be useful, or believe to be beautiful.'

Look around your home and apply this rule to everything you see. Is it useful? Do you find it beautiful? Be very honest. This exercise is only for your benefit. Nobody's going to force you to throw away all your possessions. Just go around with a pen and paper and carry out an honest assessment of everything you've purchased over the years. While you're at it, make a note of how long these things have been in your possession. You will begin to see the true value of things: some will seem more precious than you thought; others will reveal themselves as worthless.

You may find yourself asking, 'Why on earth did I buy that?' If there is anything you're not sure about, anything that is definitely not beautiful but you suspect might be useful, ask yourself how long you've had it and when you last used it.

Morris's philosophy is a good way of distinguishing between want and need. The trouble is, the distinction is constantly being blurred by the mass of misinformation that bombards us every waking hour. The language used is designed to fool us into thinking that mere 'wants' are actually 'needs'. Take the term 'must-have'. This insidious expression couldn't be more explicit in its purpose: to create the impression that the product in question is something you can't do without.

Funnily enough the expression is never applied to real essentials: on the contrary, it almost always refers to things we could very easily do without.

The world's landfill sites are full of 'must-haves', all of which have proven to be things we didn't need.

JUNK-SPENDING IS THE PURCHASE OF ANYTHING YOU DON'T NEED.

HI-TECH TOYS

When the iPhone became the 'must-have' gadget of the decade, the joke went as follows:

Q: *How do you know if someone's got an iPhone?*
A: *They tell you.*

Such is the perceived importance of owning these things that we find ourselves bragging about it.

The Digital Revolution is held up as evidence of man's increasing intelligence and sophistication. We wonder how we ever functioned without the internet or the mobile phone. But while these inventions have become hugely popular – and apparently essential – in a fairly short time, they are of less importance than the inventions of a century ago. Over a similar period spanning the late 19th century and the early 20th century, we developed the motorcar, the electric light bulb, the telephone, air travel, cinema and television.

By comparison, the Digital Revolution is simply a scaling-down and a speeding-up of our tools of communication. Not so much a revolution as a refinement, with added toys. The big concern for the digital technology industry now is that it is grinding to a halt. No one has come up with a new, breakthrough way of communicating since text messaging. They've refined the tools and added gimmicks, but each step forward is smaller than the one before.

Next time a friend or colleague turns up with the latest phone, watch them closely and try to identify any way in which their life has improved as a result of their new toy and how many of its new applications they actually use. Then decide whether you need one.

FILLING THE VOID

I've explained about the void and how it is created from birth. The comfort we seek from the moment we're born makes us vulnerable to disillusionment and insecurity. These feelings create a void, an emptiness, that needs to be filled.

But why do we try to fill the void by buying things? Why do we believe that a new watch, say, will cure our feelings of insecurity and disillusionment? The simple answer is that we are told they will. And it's not just the advertisers and marketing people who feed us with this lie. The first and most powerful influence comes from our own parents.

Is it any wonder that we try to make ourselves feel better by buying things when we grow up seeing our parents doing exactly the same? They might preach to us about the virtues of spending wisely, but the next minute they go and splash out on some new purchase and it's the most excited we've seen them all week.

When we're good, how do they reward us? By buying us things, like sweets or ice cream. I'm not saying it's wrong to buy your child an ice cream. I just want you to see how this pattern of behaviour establishes the misconception that spending and happiness somehow go hand in hand.

Think back to the happy occasions in your own childhood. Were you happy because of the ice cream or because your parents were happy with you, making you feel good about yourself?

Once you stop to think about it, it's obvious. The trouble is we're not encouraged to think about it that way. Instead, other influences step in to make us think erroneously that it was the ice cream that made us happy.

If there is only one voice in our ear and that voice is speaking authoritatively, we tend not to question it. That's why the advertising industry employs famous people to sell its wares. If someone we regard as beautiful tells us this shampoo will make us beautiful too, we believe it. If someone we regard as clever tells us this newspaper will tell us everything we need to know, we believe it.

IF SOMEONE WE REGARD AS HONEST TELLS US THIS INVESTMENT IS SOUND, WE BELIEVE IT

That's how the finance industry got away with the biggest con in history. It may not be the case any more, but when someone in a suit, representing a well-known bank or pension company, told you they would take good care of your money and make it grow, you tended to believe them. We didn't know then that the banking industry had become riddled with irresponsible gamblers, who cared only about their own profits and spared not a moment's thought for the people whose money they were gambling with.

We know now.

The lesson we've learned from the banking crisis is to question everything and everybody. 'Let the buyer beware!' Don't trust somebody on the basis of appearance. It's the oldest trick in the book. Remember, everything we're sold is dressed up to look like it's for the buyer's benefit, whether it's a packet of sweets or a self-certified mortgage. Ask what exactly it is you're being sold, make them tell you about the risks, and ask yourself, 'Do I *need* it?'

CHOOSE TO ESCAPE

We start off influenced by the behaviour of our parents, then we're dazzled by the illusions of the marketing industry and as we mature we invest our trust in people who we've been led to believe are beyond reproach. All of these influences encourage us to spend, and in believing that spending is the route to happiness, we lose control.

But wait! Didn't I begin by saying we have a choice about everything we buy?

Yes I did, and it's true, but until you understand that you have a choice, you won't be able to exercise it, particularly since there are so many influences all around you suggesting that you don't.

Once you accept that you do have a choice, escape from the debt trap is easy. Just like the optical illusion in Chapter 4, once you see things as they really are, it's impossible to see them any other way.

The truth of the matter is that nobody genuinely enjoys junk-spending – people only think they do because they've been fed a constant stream of misinformation that creates a want. The small buzz you get from spending reduces that want momentarily, but then leaves you feeling more empty than before. You mistake the emptiness for a need to spend, and so you repeat the process. That's how we get hooked.

It's essential that you stop kidding yourself that junk-spending gives you pleasure. You're ready now for my fourth instruction:

FOURTH INSTRUCTION:
DISREGARD ALL ATTEMPTS TO SELL YOU
THINGS YOU DON'T NEED

SUMMARY

- **Before buying anything, ask yourself whether in fact you really need it at all.**

- **Junk spending is not a source of happiness.**

- **The illusion that it is gets us hooked.**

- **You can choose to escape, as long as you realise you really do have the choice.**

- **Disregard all attempts to sell you things you don't need.**

Chapter 10

I'M NOT A SPENDAHOLIC

IN THIS CHAPTER
•*EXCUSES* •*WHEN MONEY BECOMES GOD*
•*THE TREADMILL* •*THE ESSENTIALS FOR HAPPINESS*
•*A STEP IN THE RIGHT DIRECTION*

Different people make up different stories to try to justify their over-spending. In reality, they're all just excuses.

Like all addicts, over-spenders are always making excuses. They lie to their loved ones and to themselves. That's not because they're bad people by nature; a lot of the time they don't even realise they're doing it. That's what addiction does to you. You know you're harming yourself and those around you and so you go to incredible lengths to justify your actions.

People provide all sorts of excuses as to why they can't do anything about getting out of debt. They each think there's something special about their situation, but I've heard it all before.

'YOU'VE GOT TO LIVE A LITTLE'

You feel that if you don't spend money, life's not worth living. So you use spending as a mood changer, like an addictive drug, because you genuinely think it will make you happy. In reality it makes you increasingly miserable as it plunges you deeper and deeper into debt.

'I DESERVE IT'

You feel a sense of entitlement. You work hard – harder than those celebrities you see swanning around in flash cars and expensive clothes – so why shouldn't you have a bit of that lifestyle? You're envious and plagued with self-pity. So you go out and spend money you don't have to give yourself a lift and stop feeling deprived. However, the initial boost soon wears off and you're left feeling lower than before as the guilt and anxiety caused by your over-spending set in.

'MONEY TALKS'

You think people are impressed by extravagance. You believe that being seen to shell out money brings you respect, so you go overboard with extravagant gestures that you think will lend you status. In fact, there's nothing more pathetic than people who drive themselves further and further into the misery of debt in an attempt to present a rich image.

'NO ONE LIKES A MISER'

Perhaps, but it doesn't follow that everyone likes a spendthrift, particularly when your family sees you spending money you don't have on things you don't need.

'I HATE RICH PEOPLE'

You see money as the root of all evil and equate wealth with greed, so you spend your money as fast as you make it, if not faster, to avoid having it burn a hole in your pocket, or your soul. However, the debts that accumulate are burning a hole in your life and you become tainted by different forms of soul-destroying behaviour.

'I'M WORTHLESS'

Your self-esteem is so low and you're feeling so negative that you feel you don't deserve to have money, so you junk-spend in order to keep yourself in financial difficulty, because that's the self-image you've become comfortable with. But the reason you're so negative is because of your money worries and if you were truly comfortable in your situation you wouldn't be reading this book.

'I'M NOT GOOD WITH MONEY'

When a personal finance story comes on the news, you have to turn it off because it frazzles your brain. You tell yourself money is a great, tangled mystery that is way beyond your understanding, and so you keep your head in the sand and carry on spending regardless of the state of your finances. But you never succeed in blocking the problem from your mind and it lurks there like an ever-enlarging dark shadow over your life.

'SOMETHING WILL TURN UP'

You're living for the day when you win the lottery, inherit a fortune or land that highly paid job, hoping it will wipe out all your debts and solve all your money problems. But until that happens, you're getting your spending in now.

This is like the smoker who carries on smoking in the hope that one morning they'll miraculously wake up a non-smoker. It doesn't happen. At some point you will have to face up to the reality of the situation. The sooner you do, the easier you'll find it to clear up the mess and the sooner your life will cease to be plagued by debt.

'I'M NOT CUT OUT TO HAVE MONEY'

You think you're a special case. Perhaps you have a low-paid job, or no job, or you're divorced, or you have learning difficulties, or you're handicapped in some way. You regard yourself as one of a downtrodden group who've been condemned to live your life in debt, and so you follow suit. Get it clearly into your mind, you do not have to suffer this misery. Millions of people in the same position, who thought they could never be debt-free, have escaped, and so will you.

'I CAN'T TOUCH MY SAVINGS'

You have money that you regard as sacred – an inheritance, say, or savings – and you don't want to break into it at any cost. So you borrow money instead, and end up getting deeper into debt in order to preserve that nest egg. But the crumb of comfort you get from preserving the nest egg is soon dwarfed by the worry of being in debt.

You may well feel you can relate to more than one of these excuses for remaining in debt. We make these excuses because we know we're doing something stupid and yet feel unable to stop. So we have to try to justify our behaviour not only to other people but also to ourselves. The tragedy is that we end up believing our own lies.

THE TRUTH BEHIND THOSE EXCUSES

Have you noticed that the happiest people are free of debt, while the most miserable are those saddled with it? In fact, spending money in an attempt to buy happiness only makes you miserable.

In these celebrity-obsessed times it's easy to be fooled into thinking you're not living life to the full if you're not rich and famous. But that's an illusion. Those beaming celebs have to look happy: that's the illusion they're paid to sell. If you spend your life craving someone else's lifestyle, you will never be happy. Extravagance can be mistaken for generosity. The truth is, people feel patronised by others throwing their money around. It doesn't make them respect you, it makes them resent you. And when they realise that it's all for show and that you're spending money you don't have, they simply think you're an idiot.

Being generous with your money is fine but it's not what makes people love you. They love you for who you are, not how much you spend, and it doesn't matter if you never buy them a present in your life, as long as you give generously in other ways: your time, your appreciation, your affection, etc.

Nor is it a bad thing to have money. Money itself is neither good nor evil. It's nothing more than a tool, like a wrench. You can use a wrench to mend a child's bicycle or you can use it to cosh someone over the head. As with any tool, it's how you use money that counts.

Most people with debt problems suffer from low self-esteem. That's not because people with low self-esteem are more prone to get into debt, but because having debt problems causes low self-esteem. And the longer you remain in debt, the more uncomfortable it's going to get. When you start to reverse your descent into debt, you'll find that your self-image changes very quickly and you'll enjoy a renewed sense of self-worth.

That's the wonderful effect of taking control. Claiming not to understand money is simply abdicating responsibility because you're afraid of taking control. Protesting that you're part of a downtrodden group is the same. Get it clearly into your mind, taking control is an essential part of getting free and feeling back in control is one of the greatest bonuses of the process that we are currently going through. So cast away your fears and go for it. After all, the worst that can happen is that you don't succeed in regaining control, in which case you'll be no worse off than you are now.

If you're waiting for a windfall to clear your debts, I'm afraid you're deluding yourself. You're considerably more likely to be struck by lightning than to win the lottery. Even if you were to receive a surprise windfall, it wouldn't solve your problem. Unless the brainwashing that has led you to over-spend is removed, you would go and spend larger amounts and it would only be a matter of time before your money worries returned.

It's surprising that anyone can get into debt when they have a nest egg in the bank, but it's not that uncommon. The fear of having nothing makes you lose the ability to think clearly about money and you make poor decisions. You take on new debts to service old ones, all the time deluding yourself that as long as you can see your pot of money sitting there untouched, everything will be all right.

But debt grows faster than credit and your nest egg is soon overshadowed by the size of your borrowings.

You know you should do something about it but you're afraid to even attempt to take control, fearing you're in too deep and that it'll be too hard. **WE ARE GOING TO REMOVE YOUR FEARS SO THAT TAKING CONTROL BECOMES EASY.**

WHEN MONEY BECOMES GOD

Our society suffers from a misunderstanding of the purpose of money. It's not surprising, because we're given so many mixed messages. In my youth the old adage was: 'Take care of the pennies and the pounds will take care of themselves.' It was a message advocating careful spending. These days the general attitude seems to be more along the lines of: 'You can't take it with you.'

Please get this straight in your mind: you can be careful with it or reckless, money itself will not make you happy. In order to understand the true purpose and value of money, you have to strip away the mass of brainwashing you've been bombarded with all your life.

Wealth has become God. Every day the media tell us about bankers and their bonuses, oligarchs and their yachts, film stars and their lavish parties.

Everybody you see on TV appears to be loaded. Their wealth is shoved in your face and if you're not living the high life, you feel a failure. The motto 'Greed is good', which was coined as a parody in the 1987 film *Wall Street*, seems to have been taken literally by investment bankers and others who crave their massive wealth. Working for job satisfaction rather than wealth is seen as weird. People are judged by the number of noughts on their pay cheque.

At the same time, happiness has become an elusive treasure. There's a rise in the incidence of eating and sleeping disorders, drug addictions and stress-related illnesses. People are so obsessed with running the rat race that they don't have time to relax. The evidence is clear for all to see: we're pursuing happiness in the wrong places.

We've been fooled into believing that money is the key. By allowing it to rule our lives, we leave ourselves vulnerable to stress, envy and misery.

THE TREADMILL

It's time for you now to step off the treadmill and escape the vicious circle. I use the term 'step off' because it really is as easy as that. You have already gone a long way towards changing your perceptions about money and debt. You now see that money is not a source of happiness and pleasure, it is merely the means by which you can acquire things. Those things should be a source of happiness and pleasure, but the money with which you buy them is nothing more than a tool, like the wrench that tightens the nut that enables a child to ride his bicycle.

In order to step off the treadmill, you need to keep an open mind. I'm going to strip away the mass of misinformation and the confusing fog of illusions that has created a society obsessed with money.

Perhaps you think I'm about to tell you to sell all your possessions and go and live in a cave. Not so. But I do want you to allow your mind to follow the exciting journey I'm about to take you on, free of confusion, pressure and stress.

IN ORDER TO SURVIVE ON THIS PLANET, THERE ARE ONLY THREE THINGS YOU NEED: FOOD, WARMTH AND SHELTER

Right now you are probably picturing a caveman wearing an animal skin and carrying a spear. Your first impression may well be negative. That's because the brainwashing has taught you to regard the caveman as a symbol of a primitive, hard, austere age.

Let me tell you about one of my happiest memories from childhood. I'm sitting alone on a rock by the sea, fishing. The sun is shining brightly and I'm in my swimming trunks. That's all I have: a fishing rod and a pair of swimming trunks and I'm as happy as can be.

To the casual observer I'm not dissimilar to the caveman, yet I'm as happy as I've ever been in my life.

Another happy memory from the same holiday is sitting in a beach hut eating my tea and gazing out to sea as a storm rolled in. I have food, I have warmth, I have shelter, and nothing else. I don't need anything else. I am content.

I'm sure there have been moments in your life when you have experienced similar happiness and I suspect that they will have taken place before you got into debt. I can't remember any such happy times when I was in debt. Funnily enough, since I got out of debt, the happy times have returned.

The point I'm making is that it's possible to be completely happy with just the three essentials of food, warmth and shelter.

A STEP IN THE RIGHT DIRECTION

You are about to stop your descent into the debt trap once and for all. From now on, whenever you find yourself in a situation where you're tempted to buy something, I want you to follow my next instruction.

FIFTH INSTRUCTION:
IF YOU CAN'T AFFORD IT, LEAVE IT

Don't worry about your existing debts for now – we will take care of those in due course. The most important thing is that you stop incurring more debts NOW. It's very simple. You have a choice. You can choose to follow my instructions and become debt-free or you can choose to continue your life of debt misery by spending money you don't have.

Don't even begin to ponder how much you might think you want or need the thing you're tempted to buy. If you can't afford it, leave it. Forget your cheque book, your credit card, debit card or store card. Just leave it.

And at that moment, instead of thinking, 'I can't have it' or 'I mustn't have it', say to yourself, 'Isn't it marvellous, I don't need to over-spend any more and I don't want to over-spend any more. Thank goodness I'm free!'

Rejoice that you're now back in control of your life. Congratulate yourself on what you have achieved. You've stepped off the treadmill of misery, not by making a sacrifice but merely by choosing not to do something that has been making you miserable. You should feel relieved and delighted. Remind yourself that the elation you feel is due to the fact that you have *not* spent. When was the last time spending made you feel this happy?

IF YOU FOLLOW THOSE INSTRUCTIONS, YOU WILL TAKE A VERY SIGNIFICANT STEP FORWARD IN GETTING OUT OF DEBT. You will prove to yourself that saying no to over-spending does not make you feel deprived or miserable; on the contrary, it gives you a boost every time as it reminds you how you've escaped from the trap that was ruining your life.

THIS IS NO TIME FOR DOOM OR GLOOM. THIS IS A TIME TO CELEBRATE SOMETHING MARVELLOUS THAT WILL TRANSFORM THE QUALITY OF YOUR LIFE

SUMMARY

- Society misunderstands the purpose of money.
- If you believe money is all-powerful, you will always be its slave.
- It's easy to step off the treadmill – you just take one step in the right direction.
- If you can't afford something, leave it.
- Stop incurring any new debts from today.

Chapter 11

THE THREE ESSENTIALS

IN THIS CHAPTER
•*HAPPINESS* •*LIFE BEFORE MONEY* •*AWAY FROM IT ALL*
•*THE BALANCE OF WEALTH* •*FOOD AND HUNGER*
•*WARMTH AND FASHION* •*SHELTER AND STATUS*

There are only three things that are essential to our physical survival. Understanding that will help to put the rest of your spending into perspective.

We've established that when it comes to surviving on this planet, there are only three things that we really need: food, warmth and shelter. But you're probably thinking that a life in which we limit our ambition to just those three essentials is not the kind of life you want to lead. You imagine a caveman hunting for food, rubbing sticks together to make fire and hunkering down in a cave and you struggle to see any appeal in that way of life. After all, haven't we spent the last half a million years evolving from that!

BUT WHEN IT COMES TO BEING HAPPY, HOW MUCH HAVE WE EVOLVED REALLY?

In the last chapter I described how one of the happiest memories from my childhood was of sitting on a rock in the sea trying to catch fish. It's really no different from the caveman in his animal skin hunting for food. I had all I needed to be happy – and all I had was a pair of swimming trunks and a fishing line.

Because the sun was shining, I didn't want for warmth or shelter, and because I'd had lunch, I didn't want for food. Because I was so engrossed in what I was doing, and so comfortable in the moment, I didn't feel any pangs of hunger all afternoon. Yet on other occasions, when I wasn't so happy, I would have started asking for an ice cream before my lunch had even had time to settle, and I would have been wondering what was for dinner long before dinner time came.

Have you noticed how children ask for food when they're bored? When we're happy, we don't get distracted by feelings like hunger until they become genuinely pressing.

Doesn't it strike you as strange that as we become adults and acquire the means to 'treat' ourselves to more and more indulgences, we find it harder and harder to achieve the level of untainted happiness that we enjoyed as children, and that moments such as my fishing experience become increasingly rare?

Rather than keep indulging ourselves with false 'pleasures', wouldn't it be a good idea to rediscover the genuine pleasures in life?

HOW MANKIND LIVED BEFORE MONEY

From the early days of being hunter-gatherers, more sophisticated than the beasts they hunted but less fierce and powerful, our ancestors recognised the value of strength in numbers. The understanding that the survival of each of them as individuals depended on the survival of the tribe as a whole became the basis of their society. They worked together protecting, supporting and looking out for one another and they shared what they had.

There are still communities in the world today that observe this custom for sharing. In parts of Polynesia, Africa and among the Native Americans, for example, it is seen that a gift should not be kept selfishly for oneself, but passed on and around, the act of giving then bringing pleasure to all, in a cycle that goes around forever.

It's a simple notion, but one that most of us, especially in the so-called developed world, sneer at. It has become our custom to put ourselves first, to cling jealously to our possessions and to put ourselves under immense pressure to get more.

Don't get me wrong, I'm sure our ancient ancestors knew the meaning of stress. Many were under pressure every day to find sustenance.

That's a real pressure; it's not the kind you can put off. Most of the pressures we feel in modern society are not real, they are perceived. We worry about things that *might* go wrong, about what people *might* say, about how we *might* feel.

CONCENTRATE ON THE THREE ESSENTIALS, FOOD, WARMTH AND SHELTER, AND THESE PERCEIVED PRESSURES PALE INTO INSIGNIFICANCE

AWAY FROM IT ALL

If we do feel overly stressed, what do we tend to do to relieve it? We get away from it all. We get out of town and head for the countryside or the sea. We leave concrete and crowds behind and go in search of wide open spaces. Some people even leave their clothes behind!

Don't worry, I'm not about to tell you that naturism is the answer to your debt problem! But doesn't this suggest that we have a natural aversion to the commercial hustle and bustle of the city and that the real pleasures in life, the ones that our natural instincts draw us towards, given half a chance, are things like sunshine, water, grass, trees, mountains, peace and quiet?

And what do we do to relax on holiday? Do we seek out the nearest internet café so that we can keep up to date with the social network? Do we find a shopping centre and spend our holidays riffling through the racks? Do we find the nearest television and lie there gazing at the screen for days on end?

Of course we don't! We get outside, we walk, we swim, we play on the beach, we read books, we enjoy the sunshine and the view, we wear simple clothes and at night we sit out and gaze at the stars. You don't have to be a naturist to appreciate that one of the great pleasures of getting away from it all is not having to worry about what you wear. Just throw on a pair of shorts and a T-shirt and you're ready to go.

The pleasures I have described are all the sort of thing you see in any brochure selling dream holidays. You might think you can't afford a dream holiday. Yet how much does any of it cost? I have tried to avoid the old cliché, 'The best things in life are free', but the more you think about it, the more you realise it's true. Can you tell me what any of the following cost:

Sunshine

Water

Grass

Trees

Mountains

Peace and quiet

Walking

Swimming

Reading a book

Looking at a view or the night sky

The only reason you might have for regarding these simple things as expensive pleasures is because they have been packaged up and sold for a very high price, because people are prepared to pay good money for them. In short, we value them very highly.

These pleasures give us the freedom to unwind, to clear our heads of all the pressures that we accumulate during our daily lives. It's only when we get the space to think like this that we realise how much junk we carry around in our heads most of the time.

THE ORIGINS OF MONEY

You might be surprised to learn that money was not invented for the purpose of trade. The word 'pay' derives from the Latin 'pacare', which means to pacify, or appease, and money first came into use as a means of paying compensation, tribute or tax. If you committed a violent crime you were obliged to pay compensation to the victim's family. Similarly, if you married, you were obliged to compensate the bride's father for depriving the family of her services. Money was also used to pay tribute to a ruler, and to pay his taxes.

It was only later, once a system of giving valuable tokens, such as decorative metals and stones, as a convenient means of payment had been established, that the same system was used to replace the rather cumbersome practice of barter. Instead of taking a cow to market to exchange for food, you could now stroll down the lane with a purse full of metal discs.

Thus money began to take on a power of its own and became disconnected from its true worth. Its value became purely representative, and so we stopped using silver and gold and used paper instead. These days, we rarely even bother with that. Our trading power – or lack of it – is recorded in binary code on a computer and accessed by way of a magnetic strip on a small piece of plastic.

TO HAVE AND HAVE NOT

Once money became a tool for oiling the wheels of commerce, it became a source of power and hence the object of greed. The world was divided into the haves and the have-nots, the former amassing more money than they knew how to spend, the latter being left to starve.

Today the distribution of the world's riches is appallingly out of balance. A tiny 1% of the adult population owns 40% of the wealth. The poorest 50% is left to share just 1% of the world's assets. So let the greedy worry about accumulating vast riches to squander on consumer products that don't make them happy. Most people have more real concerns.

And yet we are all encouraged every day to aspire to the lifestyle of that wealthy 1%. The advertising industry creates a culture of envy: 'Wouldn't you like to have what they've got?' We become brainwashed by these messages and lose sight of the things that make us truly happy. The basic pleasure of getting away from it all is packaged up and sold back to us in the form of luxury holidays. We stretch ourselves to afford them and land up in debt.

ONCE YOU ACCEPT THAT THERE ARE ONLY THREE ESSENTIALS FOR SURVIVAL, IT'S EASY TO ACCEPT THAT EVERYTHING ELSE IS A MATTER OF PERSONAL CHOICE

THE FIRST ESSENTIAL

You don't need me to tell you that food and water are essential. Go without either for just a day and our functions begin to deteriorate. Go without water for five days and you'll probably die. And while it's possible to survive for a month or more without food, it's an agonizing and rapidly debilitating experience.

Our health is inextricably linked to our intake of food and water. Most of us are well aware of this, and we recognise the tragic consequences of malnutrition in some parts of the world. Yet a bigger problem is growing out of control in other parts of the world: obesity.

In 2008, the World Health Organization predicted that by 2015 there would be 2.3 billion overweight adults in the world – roughly a third – and more than 700 million of them would be obese.

The obesity problem is evidence that we have become confused about our need for food and water in a similar way to how we've become confused about our need to spend money. It's not simply an issue of consuming too much, it's also an issue of consuming the wrong things.

Adaptability is one of the attributes that has enabled us to become the dominant species on the planet, but it has also had damaging consequences. In times of famine, when our naturally preferred foods were scarce, our ancestors adapted to living off alternatives, such as meat. More recently, we learned to use refined sugar to replicate the sweetness of the ideal food for our body, which is fresh fruit. We invented fruit flavourings and essences that fool our senses into thinking we're getting fruit, when really we're getting little more than a mouthful of saturated fat.

The trouble is that we have been brainwashed into believing that eating healthily is expensive. This misconception is reinforced by a paradox. While the poor in some parts of the world are emaciated because of lack of food, the poor in other parts are becoming increasingly overweight.

As long as your budget is small and you believe that junk food is the cheap option, you will over-eat and over-spend. If you want to save money on food and eat well, remember that the best way to satisfy hunger is to eat nutritious food.

Fresh fruit, vegetables, nuts and grains will give you all the nutrients you need in the quickest time, because your digestive system is designed to process them much quicker and more efficiently than meat and processed foods. They also happen to be the foods that naturally taste best.

Next time you feel peckish and fancy a snack, instead of buying a chocolate bar, go for a piece of fruit instead. Not only will it be much more satisfying and healthy, you'll also find it's about half the price! And you'll feel good about yourself for choosing it.

Shopping for dinner? Don't be tempted by those ready-made

meals that are packed with salt and sugar. For the same price you could buy enough fresh food for two delicious, healthy meals. You might have to learn some basic cooking skills, but cooking is fun when the result is delicious, healthy, satisfying food.

When perfectly intelligent people say they eat junk food because they can't afford to eat healthily, it shows just how deep the brainwashing goes. The fact is, they choose to eat junk because they've developed a craving for it.

Eating healthy food saves money

1. It costs less to buy.
2. You don't have to supplement it with more food to satisfy your hunger, or the false hunger created by the addiction to refined sugar.
3. It keeps you healthy and energetic, meaning less time off work and less money spent on medical treatment.

CRISIS? WHAT CRISIS?

2008 will go down in history as a year that brought financial crisis across the Western world. Less well-known is that it was also a year that saw excellent growing conditions and bumper harvests for a number of crops, including wheat, the world's number one foodstuff.

This continued in 2009 and 2010. If we still lived in a civilization whose greatest concern was nature and the success or failure of the harvest, these three years would have gone down in history as three of the best. Isn't it sad and absurd that when nature is smiling on us, we can't see it, because we have come to judge good times and bad times by the performance of the financial markets? It shows how disconnected from reality the financial world really is.

THE SECOND ESSENTIAL

We spend a lot of money on keeping warm. The cost of heating our homes and workplaces gets steeper year on year, while the clothes we wear have developed far beyond the basic purpose of keeping out the cold.

However, there are a number of things you can do to reduce the cost of keeping warm to a minimum. I was at a friend's house one winter and he was complaining about the latest rise in gas prices. I noticed he had his central heating on full blast, while he was sitting there in a T-shirt and shorts! I had come in wearing a sweater and was beginning to perspire. I asked him why he didn't put more clothes on and turn the heating down a few degrees. He said he liked to relax at home in shorts and a T-shirt.

To my mind he was kidding himself that he lived in the Bahamas, while spending an extortionate amount on his heating bills. That was his choice. Had he really been affected by the cost of his heating, he could have chosen to put on a few more layers.

I also noticed that every room in the house was heated to the same hot-house degree. But he was only using about three of them. And when he told me that he probably ought to insulate his loft, I almost gave up on him.

Domestic fuel is expensive, but there are a number of ways you can reduce your consumption. You can get free advice and financial help with insulating your property. You can restrict the heating and lighting to only the rooms you're using. And you can scan the market for the cheapest tariffs. Press your supplier for the best deal you can get. They often won't tell you about their best value packages unless you ask them.

Talking of clothes, it's important to dress in clothes that make you feel good about yourself, but being a slave to fashion is a mug's game. The fashion industry is very clever and very manipulative. It's constantly changing its messages, inventing new rules about beauty and style and preying on our deepest insecurities in order to make us keep buying more and more junk that we don't need, while ensuring that we can never quite catch up.

Step off the treadmill, choose your own look and stick with it for a while. After all, an item that looks good today will look just as good tomorrow, regardless of what some fashion guru says. It will save you money and time and give you your own style.

THE THIRD ESSENTIAL

For most of us, the need for shelter results in the biggest single expense of all: a roof over our heads. It's no surprise that in 2008 a crisis in the property market brought about the most calamitous financial collapse the Western world had seen in 80 years, because the property market is built on a staggering level of debt.

People who never dream of letting their bank account go into the red think nothing of borrowing hundreds of thousands of pounds to buy a house. The people who profit most from this market – the mortgage lenders – created a monster that grew way out of proportion by inventing products that seduced people into believing they could afford far more expensive homes than they really could.

We have come to expect to live in properties that are far bigger than we need and during the years leading up to the crash in 2008 mortgage lenders encouraged this to the extreme, by lending huge sums of money with little regard for the borrower's ability to repay. In their greedy determination to compete with each other for new business, which would earn them massive bonuses, bankers courted new customers with mortgage products that were so flimsy that the whole structure eventually came tumbling down.

But it wasn't the fat cats who picked up the bill, it was you and me, through higher taxes and cuts in public spending. A lot of people also lost their homes. By signing up to a lifestyle they couldn't afford, they were deprived of the third essential.

At the heart of this tragedy lay a common delusion: that the size of your home says something about who you are. Kings and queens live in palaces, paupers live in shacks. It's been the same for hundreds, if not thousands, of years, but what does it have to do with happiness? Do you need ten different rooms to be happy?

The modern trend is for one main room that serves as the heart of the home: a kitchen-cum-living room, where you cook, eat, relax, watch TV, listen to music, etc. Even in houses that were built with separate living rooms, dining rooms and kitchens, it's now common practice to knock them all into one, which goes to show just how non-essential a big house with many rooms really is. People often aspire to live somewhere like that because they believe it to be a mark of success.

But the belief that a big house amounts to a successful life is false, as false as the belief that expensive cars or a big wardrobe will bring you happiness. There's nothing wrong with living in a big house if it makes you happy. Most people think they would be happier in a bigger house, with more space to move around and more room for their possessions. But the financial pressure we put ourselves under to afford the extra space often negates any pleasure.

THE CONFUSION OF <u>EXCESS</u> WITH <u>SUCCESS</u> IS RESPONSIBLE FOR A MAJOR PART OF THE WORLD'S DEBT PROBLEMS

If you find it difficult to pay your rent, or pay the instalments on your mortgage, without having to take on more debt, ask yourself whether your home exceeds your needs. Your immediate reaction will probably be: 'No!'. But carry out an honest assessment of your everyday movements around the home and you might be surprised. There's no reason to feel ashamed about moving to somewhere cheaper to live.

It's also worth noting that 'cheaper' doesn't necessarily mean 'smaller'. Location is the main factor in deciding property values.

So if you're struggling to afford to live in your current area, doesn't that suggest that it's not the ideal location for you and you'd be happier in an area where property is more affordable?

The key is to find a balance between size, location and affordability that gives you the most happiness. If you're already in debt and have to take on more debt in order to pay for your home, it's safe to say that the balance is not right.

The good news is that, whatever your circumstances, you will be able to have a home that provides you with one of the three essential ingredients to live a happy life.

SUMMARY

- **Concentrate on the three essentials for physical survival and most of the perceived pressures in life pale into insignificance.**

- **The best things in life really are free.**

- **Let the greedy worry about money, while you focus on happiness.**

- **Remember you have a choice over what you spend.**

- **Eating healthily does NOT cost more.**

- **The confusion between excess and success is at the root of the world's debt problems.**

THE CREDIT TRAP

The credit industry relies on you being in debt and goes to great lengths to convince you that it is for your benefit.

Imagine you go into a greengrocer's to buy apples. He weighs your apples and they come to £2 worth. You pay the £2, take your apples and leave. The transaction is complete. You don't expect to keep paying for the apples month after month, do you?

But that's exactly what happens every time you use a credit card, unless you pay off your entire balance each month. Everything you buy costs more than the retail price that the shopkeeper asks, because every time you make a purchase with your credit card, you incur new debt and that debt carries a cost in the form of interest.

AND THE INTEREST RATES CHARGED ON YOUR OUTSTANDING MONTHLY BALANCE BY THE CREDIT CARD COMPANIES ARE HORRENDOUSLY HIGH

Say you'd never heard of credit cards and I tried to sell the idea to you on that basis; you would laugh in my face. 'Here, try this piece of plastic. It fits neatly inside your wallet and whenever you want to buy something, all you have to do is hand it to the shopkeeper and thereby ensure that you pay more for the goods.'

It's a ludicrous proposition, especially for someone with debt problems, who's looking for ways to pay less, not more. So why are so many people, even those already in debt, seduced by credit cards to the point where they believe they can't live without them?

Again, it comes back to marketing. The credit industry depends on customers getting themselves into debt. The deeper the debt, the more the credit companies make. They feed on the vulnerable, punish those most in need of help and have no scruples about demanding their exorbitant interest rates from those who can least afford them.

If you had to sell a business proposition like that, how would you go about it? I've never worked in marketing but I've seen enough to know that the first thing you have to do is gloss over the negatives and put a positive spin on it. And the first word that springs to a marketeer's mind in these situations is:

FREEDOM

It's a very evocative word. It's not a concept anyone in their right mind would argue against, and so it's an easy word to bandy about unchallenged. It's a word that you'll hear used in defence of all sorts of things that are indisputably bad for us, such as smoking, over-eating, alcoholism and other drug addictions. Killing ourselves, we are told, is a matter of personal freedom.

ESSENTIAL CONSIDERATIONS

The other word that marketeers love to use when selling a dodgy proposition is 'convenience'. 'Hey, this card makes it easy to buy whatever you want whenever you want. It removes all the obstacles. What could be more convenient?'

Put this way, it's an enticing proposition, isn't it? But it presupposes that the obstacles that prevent you buying something without a credit card are a bad thing.

What are those obstacles? One obvious one is not having enough money to afford it. Another is the conscious thought process you would go through before making the purchase if you did not have such easy access to money that is not yours. That thought process might well result in you deciding that the purchase is unnecessary and that you should save your money to spend on something else.

Both of these 'obstacles' are actually essential considerations in keeping out of debt. They are considerations that people who are not in debt apply all the time and they are considerations you applied quite comfortably before you fell into the credit trap. If it now causes you distress to apply them, then you should ask yourself why. We feel distress for a good reason: it's a warning sign that there's something wrong that needs to be put right. If we're suffering from pain, we may swallow a painkiller. It may take the pain away for a while but it doesn't remove the underlying problem.

Credit cards create the same false impression. They anaesthetize our brain from the thought process that protects us from getting into debt. They lure us into running up new debts by making it easy and seemingly painless.

But this is an illusion as, just like the debt itself, the underlying distress gets worse and worse. Meanwhile, the credit companies keep increasing the dose, offering higher and higher credit limits, until one day they decide you've been allowed enough, and they stop.

That's when you really feel the pain, and now it's a hundred times worse.

The name 'credit card' is part of the cunning marketing of this trap. It should be called a 'debt card', because that's exactly what it does: it encourages you to incur more debt.

It may seem to make life easier to begin with, but in the long run it causes disaster. You struggle to keep track of your spending and you find yourself suffering from the pressure of going deeper and deeper into debt. You try to block your mind to this, but it's like a dark shadow always looming at the back of your mind and as you go deeper and deeper into the trap, it just gets darker and darker.

THE LONGER YOU GO ON USING A CREDIT CARD, THE LESS AFFORDABLE EVERYTHING BECOMES. REMEMBER, CREDIT CARDS MAKE EVERYTHING MORE EXPENSIVE

FURTHER DECEPTIONS

In addition to the claims of freedom and convenience, credit companies market their products on the basis of several other illusions designed to take in their customers.

1. It's easier than cash

As I've explained, credit cards don't make life easier, they make running up debts easier. If you don't like carrying cash around, use a debit card, which gives you access to your money, but not to money you don't have.

2. It earns me respect

It's another clever marketing trick that a small rectangle of plastic should have come to represent your sense of self-worth. The notion of different types of credit cards bestowing different levels of status on their bearers is a con that preys on our innermost insecurities. 'You want to seem a person of substance? Carry a gold card.' By giving you the honour of qualifying for a gold card, they make you feel like you've been welcomed into some privileged and elite club. 'Do come in, sir. Let me take your coat, madam. And allow me to relieve you of all your money while I'm at it.' Every time you 'flash the card', they're laughing all the way to the bank, as they extract more and more money from you in the form of interest fees, for which you get precisely nothing.

3. I can handle it

Everyone who signs up for a credit card begins with the same intentions. 'I'll pay off the balance each month, no problem.' You can actually convince yourself that your new card makes sound economic sense. 'Why pay now when I can pay later and gain an extra few days' worth of interest on the money in my bank account?'

That's the theory. But the reality is that our best intentions are easily abandoned. When times get hard or we need cheering up, where do we turn?

One credit card company coined the phrase 'your flexible friend'. And many people lean on it as they would a friend, seeking comfort in spending.

The very principle of credit, i.e. 'buy now, pay later', creates a state of mind whereby 'later' becomes the key word. Gradually we defer the pain of actually paying for the things we've bought until later and later.

At first the charges seem tiny, almost imperceptible, and we don't feel threatened by them. But the more we follow this path of deferred payment, the more the debt builds up.

All credit cards, whatever their terms, create this same sense that it's OK to put off paying and encourage you into the debt trap.

4. **I need a credit card for rentals**

It's a common misconception that if you're renting a car or hiring a piece of equipment you have to have a credit card to offer as collateral, and for identification. This is not so. Most hire firms offer alternatives. It may involve making arrangements in advance, taking ID and paying the deposit by debit card or in cash, but it can be done and it's really not inconvenient.

5. **I need it for shopping online**

Online shopping is a massive growth area. It's also one that instils a lot of uncertainty. 'Just how secure is it? What if the merchant is a rogue? What's to stop them using my credit card details illegally?'

Despite these fears, millions of people shop online every day and a large number of them pay by credit card. It is generally very quick and easy. Just like using your credit card in a shop, it's a quick and easy way into debt. Using a debit card instead avoids this risk as it only draws on the money you have available at the bank.

So if you like shopping online then all you have to do is use a debit card rather than a credit card. Alternatively, you can always contact the seller and arrange an alternative method of payment, such as an online transfer from your bank or a cheque. Some will even allow you to pay cash on delivery. Remember, it's in the merchant's interest to make a sale any way they can, so they will usually be very helpful.

6. **It helps my cash flow**

This is just another way of saying, 'It allows me to buy things when I haven't got the money.' This is only going to result in one thing: debt.

If your personal finances run on a cycle whereby money comes into your bank account periodically in sufficient amounts to pay off the debts you've accrued while your account was empty, you may think a credit card is the perfect tool to help level out the peaks and troughs. But as long as you use a credit card, you will be encouraged to run up debts.

The very fact that you are able to pay off your balance when the money comes in shows that you don't need to go into debt in the first place. All you have to do is manage your finances in a different way, shifting the cycle so that your bumper periods precede your lean ones, rather than the other way round. Then you'll be able to make your money last over the period when you have no cash coming in, just as you do now, but without having to go into debt.

GOING INTO THE BLACK

We have established that everything costs more when you keep your finances in the red. This is because you have to pay interest on your debts, as well as the purchase price of what you buy.

Some people actually have an aversion to keeping their finances in the black. They feel that they're restricted, whereas once they go into the red there seem to be no restrictions. But this is another illusion. Sure, there is a restriction when you're keeping in the black: zero. That is the lower limit, below which you cannot fall if you want to stay in the black. It seems like a tough restriction to some people because they're not accustomed to keeping their finances above zero, and they fear that if they tried to they would be constantly on edge.

But there's a limit when you're in the red too: your credit limit. When you keep your finances in the red, you are still restricted by this lower limit, beyond which your 'flexible friend' will not stretch.

So what's the difference – other than the fact that when you're in the red, you pay the bank, and when you're in the black, the bank pays you?

Let's imagine two people with the same income and the same outgoings each month. Let's say they both make £1,000 a month and they both spend £1,000. Person A keeps his finances in the black, person B keeps them in the red.

On payday, A's bank account goes up from £0 to £1,000, while B's goes from –£1,000 to £0. By the following payday, A's balance has returned to £0, while B's has returned to –£1,000. However, each month the bank charges interest on minus balances and pays interest on positive balances. For the sake of simplicity, let's say the charge is £4 per month and the payment is £1.

This means that come pay day, person A has £1 in the bank, while person B has –£1,004. After a year, person A's account rises to £1,012 on pay day, while person B's only reaches –£48. Each month, while person A has become better off, person B has fallen further and further below zero.

YET BOTH HAVE THE SAME INCOME AND ARE LEADING EXACTLY THE SAME LIFESTYLE

In reality, the discrepancy is more pronounced, because as both positive and negative balances move further away from zero, so the interest payments increase. Simply by keeping his account in the red, person B becomes rapidly worse off than person A.

As time goes on, the gap grows exponentially. The £1,000 monthly spending is augmented by interest charges, which in turn increase the debt the following month, and so the whole thing snowballs.

> 'Debt: *an ingenious substitute for the chain and whip of the slavedriver.'*
> - Ambrose Bierce

It's possible to go on living in the red for a long time by adopting a 'head-in-the-sand' approach to the escalating catastrophe of your financial situation. Living on credit may seem relatively painless until the creditors want their money back.

That's when you're forced to take your head out of the sand and accept that debt has been gnawing away at the foundations of your world like woodworm, and the whole lot risks crashing down.

It's vital, therefore, that you begin to manage your finances like person A. In the next chapter we are going to take the first simple steps towards achieving that. If you've understood everything you've read so far, your attitude towards over-spending, junk-spending and remaining in debt will have changed, the door to your prison will have been unlocked and the time has come to start the practical process of becoming debt-free. If you have any doubts or confusion about anything I have mentioned here, go back and re-read from Chapter 4 onwards.

Above all, keep an open mind and rejoice that you're breaking free from the misery of debt. There's nothing to fear, you don't need willpower and there's nothing peculiar to you that can prevent you from escaping. Now that's something to celebrate!

SUMMARY

- Credit cards make things more expensive.
- The credit industry thrives on debt – the worse your debt, the more money they make.

- Living life in the red makes you exponentially poorer.
- Congratulations! You are ready to bring your debt problems to an end.

Chapter 13

NOTHING TO FEAR

IN THIS CHAPTER

•*WHAT YOU'VE ACHIEVED SO FAR*
•*TIME TO MAKE A NEW CHOICE* •*KNOW YOUR ENEMY*

As you stand on the brink of ending your debt problem, cast aside any lingering fears and remember the truths you have discovered. Rejoice! You are about to walk free!

I ended the last chapter by saying that you are about to take your first step towards getting out of debt. In fact, you have already taken your first steps. Opening this book was your first positive step. And now you have come a long way towards achieving the state of mind necessary for you to quit incurring new debts and to turn the tide, so that you can get out of the red and into the black.

Congratulate yourself on your achievements so far. Remind yourself that there is no need to feel miserable; on the contrary, you have every reason to feel excited. You're releasing yourself from a prison that has brought you nothing but stress and misery and you're choosing a life that will bring you more happiness than you can imagine.

Perhaps you think you have no reason to congratulate yourself. Maybe you feel you haven't achieved anything yet. Your debts haven't got any smaller, your lifestyle hasn't changed and you're still struggling to convince yourself that this is going to be as easy as I say. **IT'S TIME TO ADDRESS THE FEAR OF SUCCESS.**

We established earlier that the fear of life outside jail can keep the prisoner trapped. He feels secure in his prison because it's an environment he knows. Even though it's a life of slavery, he fears it less than the world outside, which is alien and riddled with uncertainty.

In the context of getting out of debt, we have also established that the fear of success is caused by illusions. These illusions have been put in our brain by many influences, which have a vested interest in us being in debt.

You've been fooled into believing that spending money somehow makes you attractive, that it wins respect and makes you happy.

You also fear that getting out of debt will be hard, maybe too hard to bear. You fell into debt easily but assume it will be incredibly difficult to climb out, as if debt were a hole in the ground covered with branches and leaves into which you stumbled unwittingly and now find yourself in above your head.

But that's not the case. Though it may feel like a deep, dark hole, there's no physical effort required to escape. You simply need to make a choice. It's a simple choice between taking a step backwards or a step forwards. You can either choose to remain in the debt trap for the rest of your life, going deeper and deeper into it, becoming more and more enslaved and miserable, or you can choose freedom.

You were lured into debt by the illusions peddled to you by people with a vested interest. They either had an interest in you spending money regardless of whether you could afford to, or they had an interest in you having to borrow.

You took a step backwards. And you've found that you can't handle it. So now you just have to choose to do the opposite. Take a step forward. It's as simple as that. However, perhaps you still have fears.

Some of our fears are instinctive. For example, the fear of heights, fire or the sea are instinctive responses that protect us from falling, getting burnt or drowning. There's nothing instinctive about the fear of getting out of the debt trap.

THE FEAR OF GETTING OUT OF THE DEBT TRAP IS BASED ON ILLUSIONS

DON'T BANK ON BANKRUPTCY

You will no doubt have heard accounts of people who fell heavily into debt but were able to declare themselves bankrupt and have all their debts wiped out by the courts. Perhaps you think this is your ideal solution: wipe the slate clean and begin again from scratch, making sure you're more careful this time.

Forget it!

More than half the people who go bankrupt will do

so again. Bankruptcy solves nothing for them because it does not tackle the real problem: their addiction to over-spending. As soon as they are legally permitted, they start running up debts again.

Remember, our aim is to remove the brainwashing that is the real cause of your debt problem. Declaring yourself bankrupt can do untold damage to your self-esteem and confidence, which in turn will sabotage the positive mentality you need to overcome your addiction.

The only sensible way to solve your debt problem painlessly and permanently is to face up to the fact that you are in a trap and allow this book to show you the way out.

YOU'RE IN CONTROL

Once you're free from the debt trap, you'll be amazed at how easy it was to escape, you'll lead a far happier life and your only regret will be not having made your escape sooner. At the moment you may still feel like someone trapped at the bottom of a deep pit, unable to see a way out. But once you get out, you'll realise there was no pit. All you had to do was take a step forward instead of a step back. It's as simple as that.

In order to achieve success you need to remove all doubt. You must understand and accept that any fears you may have about trying to become debt-free are based on illusions. In reality, you have nothing to fear.

Perhaps you question whether it's possible to know for certain that something will *not* happen, i.e. even if you do manage to become debt-free, how do you know you won't fall into the trap again. After all, the chances of being struck by a meteorite are infinitesimally small, yet nobody can say with absolute certainty that it will never happen to them.

That's true; however, you have a considerable advantage over potential meteorite victims: if a meteorite is going to hit you, there's nothing you can do about it, whereas only you can make yourself go back to over-spending. You are in control and once you've seen through the confidence trick that lured you into debt in the first place, you will never be taken in again.

If you still have doubts and fears at this stage, don't worry, that's perfectly normal. You've been brainwashed into thinking you have to make huge sacrifices to get out of debt; that the process will be hard and miserable; and that, even if you do succeed, you will be forever tempted to get back into debt again. These are illusions. Once you're in the right frame of mind and start applying the simple steps that I am going to take you through, you will change your perception and the fear will go.

My second instruction was to keep an open mind. If you have followed this instruction, you will realise by now that the fears you had about getting out of debt were baseless and brought about by brainwashing, and so they were not genuine concerns at all. If you did not follow this instruction, I urge you to go back and read it through again, making sure you allow your mind to take it on board.

In order to undo the brainwashing, you need to realise that you have been brainwashed and understand how that brainwashing has distorted the truth. Then you can see things as they really are.

Remember the STOP diagram in Chapter 4? If I hadn't told you that there was another message there, you might never have recognised it. But as soon as I told you there was another message, you quickly saw it. And once you'd seen it, you couldn't fail to see it every time.

ONCE YOU SEE THINGS AS THEY REALLY ARE, YOU CAN NEVER BE DELUDED AGAIN

NO GET-OUT CLAUSE

Once they realise that fear is the only thing preventing them from quitting, some addicts try to allay their fear by telling themselves they can always relapse if it gets too hard; it doesn't have to be final. Start with that attitude and you will almost certainly fail. Instead, start with the certainty that you are going to find it easy to succeed.

TIME TO TAKE CONTROL

You have already come a long way in the process of unravelling the brainwashing that has kept you in debt and putting yourself in the right frame of mind to escape the prison. Now you are going to start taking the practical forward steps that will get you into the black.

Your first positive step was choosing to read this book. You had a choice: to bury your head in the sand and continue going further and further into debt, or to take positive action to resolve the situation. You made a positive choice. All I ask is that you continue making positive choices.

As we move forward, there are three very important facts that I want you to remember:

1. Junk-spending does absolutely nothing for you at all.
It is crucial that you understand this so that you never get a feeling of deprivation.

2. There is no need for a transitional period.
With drug addicts this is often referred to as the 'withdrawal period'. But anyone who quits with my method has no need to worry about the withdrawal period. Yes, it will take time to clear your debts, but the moment you stop running up new ones is the moment you become free. You don't have to wait for anything to happen.

3. There is no such thing as 'just this once' or 'the occasional spree'.
Any amount of junk-spending must be seen for what it is: part of a lifelong chain of self-destruction.

WILL IT MAKE ME A MISER?

Perhaps you think that I'm going to advocate that you stop spending altogether and start hoarding your money. No. Misers tend to be miserable, and my whole objective is to help you free yourself from misery.

Generosity is a great source of happiness. Once you've quit junk-spending, you will find that you have more money to spend not only on yourself but also on others and you will gain much more from the money you do spend.

And remember point 1 above: junk-spending does absolutely nothing for you. It is not a source of happiness. You don't have to spend money to be happy. The best things in life are free.

Practical steps

Take a pen and paper and write down all the activities that give you genuine pleasure in a month. Really think about it. Take a day or two over it if you like, and write down the things you enjoy as they come to mind. Focus on the times when you feel most relaxed and happy, and when your debts are furthest from your mind. This will help you to become aware of what you really enjoy and value in life. Your list might look something like this:

Seeing friends	Going to the cinema
Going for a walk	Taking part in sport
Going for a bike ride	Watching sport
Having a nice meal	Gardening
Reading	Listening to music

KNOW YOUR ENEMY

Many addicts suffer the illusion that they can never get completely free. They convince themselves that their addiction is their friend, their confidence, their support, even part of their identity. And so they fear that if they quit, they will not only lose their closest companion, they will lose a part of themselves.

It's a stark indication of just how deeply the brainwashing distorts reality that anyone should come to regard something that is destroying them and making them miserable as a friend.

When you lose a friend, you grieve. Eventually you come to terms with the loss and life goes on, but you're left with a genuine void in your life that you can never fill. There's nothing you can do about it. You have no choice but to accept the situation and, though it still hurts, you do.

When smokers, alcoholics, heroin users and other addicts try to quit by willpower, they feel they're losing a friend. They know that they're making the right decision to stop, but they still suffer a feeling of sacrifice and, therefore, there's a void in their lives. It isn't a genuine void but they believe it is, and so the effect is the same. They feel as if they're mourning for a friend. Yet this false friend isn't even dead. The purveyors of drugs and debt make absolutely sure that these tortured souls are forever subjected to the temptation of forbidden fruit for the rest of their lives.

However, when you rid yourself of your mortal enemy, junk-spending, there is no need to mourn. On the contrary, you can rejoice and celebrate from the start, and you can continue to rejoice and celebrate for the rest of your life.

THAT'S WHY IT'S VITAL TO GET IT CLEAR IN YOUR MIND THAT JUNK-SPENDING IS NOT YOUR FRIEND, NOR IS IT PART OF YOUR IDENTITY

It never has been. In fact, it's your worst enemy and by getting rid of it you're sacrificing absolutely nothing, just making marvellous, positive gains.

So the answer to the question, 'When will I be free?' is, 'Whenever you choose to be'.

You could spend the next few days, and possibly the rest of your life, continuing to believe that junk-spending was your friend and wondering when you'll stop missing it. If you do that, you will just feel miserable, the desire to junk-spend may never leave you and you'll either end up feeling deprived for the rest of your life, or you'll end up going back to junk-spending and feeling even worse.

Alternatively, you can recognise junk-spending for the mortal enemy that it really is and take pleasure in cutting it entirely out of your life. Then you need never crave it again, and whenever the idea enters your mind, you will feel elated that it's no longer ruining your life.

Unlike people who quit with the willpower method, you'll be happy to think about your old enemy and you needn't try to block it from your mind. Trying not to think about something is a sure way of becoming obsessed with it. If I tell you not to think about elephants, what's the first thing that comes into your head? Exactly!

In fact, there's no reason to try not to think about it. On the contrary, enjoy thinking about it and rejoice that it no longer plagues your life.

Think back to the case of person A and person B in the last chapter, both leading the same lifestyle, both on the same income, but person A keeping his account in the black, person B in the red. Our objective is to help you enjoy life like person A.

In order to achieve that, we need to remove all temptation to run up any more debts.

The last chapter explained how credit cards do nothing for you except encourage you further into debt. Despite all the promises, they do not give you freedom or convenience. Quite the opposite! They make life more expensive and trap you in a vicious circle that plunges you further and further into debt as interest charges increase exponentially and the amount you owe becomes a burden that threatens your wellbeing.

DESPITE THE POPULAR MYTH, IT'S EASY TO LIVE WITHOUT A CREDIT CARD

Soon I am going to ask you to destroy your credit cards. Once you've done so, you will find it easy not to incur any new debts. And once you realise that you have the power to stop incurring new debts, you will feel a wonderful sense of freedom.

REAL FREEDOM

SUMMARY

- Debt is not a hole in the ground – there is no physical effort required to get out.

- It's easy to get out of debt – you just have to think differently about how you choose to spend your money.

- Have no doubts about the choice you are making and be certain that you will succeed.

- Remember, junk-spending does nothing for you at all.

- There's nothing to wait for. The moment you stop over-spending is the moment you become free.

- There's no such thing as 'the occasional spree' – all junk-spending is part of a chain of misery.

- Rejoice at ridding yourself of your mortal enemy.

Chapter 14

TAKING CONTROL

IN THIS CHAPTER

• *NEGATIVE ARGUMENTS* • *DENIAL*

• *THE TURNING POINT*

• *YOUR FINAL DEBT*

Congratulations! The time has come to end your debt problem.

Though they may deny it even to themselves, people in debt know that they're not in control of their spending. That's not to say they're all the type of people who struggle to keep control over everything. On the contrary, many are very good at managing other aspects of their life, such as work or social activities. And yet for some reason that they can't get to the bottom of, they find it impossible to get on top of their finances.

This leaves them feeling a slave to money and makes them frustrated, angry, powerless and miserable. It takes courage to admit that you have a problem and to do something positive about tackling it. The simple act of seeking help – in your case picking up this book – is the first in a series of simple steps that will bring an end to your debt problem.

Such is the nature of the debt trap that people don't realise just how powerless they have become until they have escaped the trap and rediscovered their sense of true freedom and happiness. So intent are we on resisting the need to face our debt problem that we try to block our mind to the terrible effects it has on our lives. But we never quite succeed in doing so, and the anxiety lurks at the back of our mind like a black shadow, which gets larger and larger and darker and darker the more we spiral into debt.

Asked why we spend money on things we don't need, our reaction is nearly always defensive and negative. We can't seem to find reasons why we do it, but instead we resort to reasons why we haven't stopped doing it.

'I've got it under control.'

'It's a free country.'

'There are worse things in life.'

'It's not hurting anybody.'

Wait a minute, don't we junk-spend because we think it gives us pleasure and makes us happy? Now, I regard a round of golf as a pleasure, but if anybody asked me why I play so much golf, I wouldn't respond by saying, 'I've got it under control' or 'It's a free country'. I would tell them all the positive reasons why I play golf, all the pleasures I get from it: the fresh air, the scenery, the exercise, the sociability, the challenge, etc. When something gives you genuine pleasure, you're only too keen to enthuse about it. You don't make excuses for why you don't stop doing it!

One aim of this book is to reverse all the brainwashing that has kept you in debt until now. What really sets you free is the realization that you don't need to be a slave to money or junk-spending. You won't feel deprived, you will enjoy life more, you will handle stress better and you won't have to go through any terrible trauma in order to become debt-free.

OVERCOMING DENIAL

The pressure and helplessness that come with debt problems tend to make us close our minds to reality. The further we get into debt, the more we feel that the truth is too horrible to face, so we push it to the back of our mind and kid ourselves that life can carry on as it is.

Yet, try as we might, we can never completely block the problem from our mind. It makes us miserable, defensive, evasive, angry and stressed and yet we're too afraid to face up to it because we feel there's no solution.

I have asked you to read this book with an open mind. The mind of people in debt is often closed, making it impossible for them to see the easy way out of the trap. But escape is as simple as taking a step forward rather than a step back. Once you open your mind and recognise that nothing genuinely stands in your way, it becomes easy.

In reality, there is nothing to fear. On the contrary, you have everything to gain. In order to become free, you need to determine the extent of your debts.

THE EXTENT OF YOUR DEBTS

Take a pen and paper and sit down at a table. Take a deep breath. Relax. Now make a list of all the ways in which you've incurred new debts over the past twelve months. This could be anything from borrowing £10 from a friend on a night out to putting a holiday on your credit card. Think about it carefully. Don't forget the store cards, the bank loans and the finance deals. Be honest with yourself. This is for your eyes only – it's nothing to be ashamed of. What is important is that you recognise the scale of your debt and accept it as fact.

Now make another list, of all the times you've fallen behind with your repayments on these loans. If there are other debts that you incurred more than a year ago but have missed payments on in the last twelve months, add those to the list. You may have to do a little research to find these details. One of the ironies of being in debt is that you tend not to have a clear idea of where your money goes.

I'm sure you've experienced that feeling on a Sunday morning, when you look in your wallet and wonder where your cash has gone. You took out £50 on Saturday night, spent £25 on a meal, £5 on something to drink, £10 on a cab home and now you've got nothing. Somewhere along the line you've mislaid £10 but you have no idea where. The likelihood isn't that you lost it, but that you either spent it on something you can't remember or haven't recalled the amounts accurately.

The denial of being in debt means this sort of thing happens all the time. You can't keep track of everything you spend because that would mean facing up to the full horror of your financial situation. So you take a casual approach and, surprise surprise, money goes missing.

IT'S TIME TO BECOME COMPLETELY AWARE OF WHERE ALL YOUR MONEY GOES

THE TURNING POINT

We are at the turning point in your debt problem, the point at which you begin to reverse the flow of your finances.

Imagine you're walking along a path through a forest. All the time you have been increasing your debts you have been walking in the wrong direction and the forest has been growing denser and denser all around you. You can't actually see the way out, but you know that logically all you need to do is turn around and start walking in the opposite direction. At the point between walking the wrong way and walking the right way is a moment when you stop. You are neither moving one way nor the other. This is where you are now. This is the turning point.

Very soon you will start walking in the right direction. But first you need to stop walking deeper into the forest. In other words, you need to stop taking on new debts. Forget about your existing debts or the interest payments on them for the moment. Once you've reached the turning point and started walking out of the forest, they will be dealt with painlessly. The important thing is to stop incurring any new debts now.

YOUR FINAL DEBT

But first, I want you to over-spend on junk one last time. Take your credit card or store card, walk into any shop you choose and buy something you don't need with money you don't have. As you hand the card to the cashier, focus on how you're feeling. Is it giving you pleasure? Does it make you feel good?

As you punch your PIN into the card reader, concentrate on

your emotions. Is this expenditure giving you a buzz? Is it making you happy?

When you get home with your purchase, unpack it and hold it. Are you happy with it? Be aware of exactly how this purchase has made you feel. Stripped of the brainwashing that previously told you this sort of spending gave you pleasure, you can recognise what an empty, meaningless act it is to spend money you don't have on something you don't need.

Remember, you can't get out of debt by borrowing more money, any more than a junkie can get clean by injecting more heroin. You have a simple choice. Whenever it occurs to you to spend money that means going further into debt: STOP.

It's not difficult and without any credit cards it's even easier because the simplest course of borrowing will no longer be an option. Your mind will then be free to weigh up just how much you need the thing you're considering buying.

If it really is something you need, use your imagination to come up with a way to get it, or a substitute for it that will do the same thing, that does not mean getting further into debt. Perhaps you could borrow the item from a friend. Perhaps it means waiting a little to get it or cutting out some other expenditure – so what? That's what people who aren't in debt do all the time and it doesn't make them miserable, stressed, frightened or antisocial.

Taking away the temptation to incur new debts is as easy as cutting a piece of plastic in half with a pair of scissors. It requires the minimum of physical effort. It will only seem hard if you still regard that plastic as valuable. If you still think your credit cards represent freedom and convenience, please go back and re-read Chapter 12. The sooner you accept that 'credit' is just a trap designed to keep you in debt for the rest of your life, the sooner you will turn your finances around.

The moment you stop borrowing is the turning point. And the first thing you can do to stop borrowing is to destroy the plastic that makes it so easy and mindless. You're now ready for my sixth instruction.

SIXTH INSTRUCTION:

DESTROY ALL YOUR CREDIT CARDS AND STORE CARDS AND REMOVE ANY OTHER SOURCES OF DEBT

Cast aside your fears and any feelings of doom or gloom. Get it clearly into your mind: nothing bad is happening; you are not making a sacrifice and there is no reason to feel deprived. On the contrary, you are doing something marvellous for yourself and for your life. Cut through that plastic with relish and enjoy dumping the source of so much misery in the rubbish bin for good.

You also need to make sure you don't borrow money from any other sources. No more cheques from an account that you know not to have sufficient funds; no borrowing from friends or family or, much worse, loan sharks; no IOUs; nothing.

Whenever you find yourself in a situation where you would have written a cheque or handed over your credit card, instead of feeling like you're somehow missing out, think, 'Isn't this marvellous! I don't have to incur any new debts.'

TIMING

Perhaps you're wondering when would be the best time to follow this instruction. Perhaps you think it's best to wait until after the weekend, or maybe there's an event coming up, such as a birthday or Christmas, which you should get out of the way before you make your move.

SEVENTH INSTRUCTION:
DO IT NOW!

The moment you stop incurring new debts is the moment you become free. Why put off such a wonderful occasion?

You need to make a solemn vow that you will never over-spend again. In order to make that vow easily, it helps to realise that there is a particular beauty about this decision. With other important decisions, such as whom we choose for a partner or what we do for a living, we can never be sure they're correct. Even if we don't regret them years later, we can never know what would have happened if we had done something else. The beauty about the decision you are currently making in your mind is that you know it's the correct decision, even as you make it. You will not be able to say that about many other vital decisions you make.

Having made what you know to be the correct decision, never even begin to question or doubt that decision. It's only the questioning or doubting of that decision that can possibly prevent you from becoming free. Congratulate yourself on achieving something wonderful. Once you have proved to yourself that you can stop over-spending, you will feel a marvellous sense of relief. And all you had to do was choose not to incur any new debts. There was no pain. In fact, it was easy.

CONGRATULATIONS! YOU NO LONGER HAVE A SPENDING PROBLEM

SUMMARY

- This is the moment when FREEDOM beckons.
- You have been taken in by the credit companies that have lured you into debt.
- But now you have a CHOICE – you can acquiesce in your own ruin OR
- YOU CAN STEP BACK FROM THE PRECIPICE AND BEGIN TO BELIEVE IN YOURSELF AGAIN.
- It takes just ONE DECISION to change your life.

Chapter 15

MAKING PLANS

IN THIS CHAPTER
•*PUT IT IN WRITING* •*SEEING IS BELIEVING* •*BALANCING THE BOOKS*
•*PRIORITIZING* •*THE PLAN TAKES SHAPE*
•*THE FOURTH ESSENTIAL* •*SACRED SAVINGS*

Now that you are out of the over-spending trap, you can begin the process of clearing your debts. Start by writing it all down.

SEEING IT IN BLACK AND WHITE

The moment you complete your final debt transaction and realise that you neither need nor want to incur a debt ever again is the moment you are free from the debt trap.

Some people find this difficult to accept. They think they can't become free until all their debts are cleared. However, once you've stopped over-spending and put in place the system that I am about to explain to you, you are certain to clear your debts and with this certainty comes freedom.

The knowledge that you have a strategy in place, which cannot fail to resolve your difficulties, means that you can stop worrying now. It's like my method for losing weight.

Once I had understood the way in which I needed to eat in order to be healthy and happy, the fact that it was going to take some time actually to lose the surplus pounds didn't bother me in the slightest. I knew I had the answer to my problem and from that moment it was solved. As the pounds dropped off, it gave me a marvellous sense of achievement and I had no need to wait until I actually reached my ideal weight to rejoice in the knowledge that my problem was over.

In the same way, you don't have to wait until you've cleared all your debts before rejoicing in the knowledge that you're free from the debt trap. In order to remain free, you need to begin a new way of managing your money, a way that will see you clear your debts and enjoy a vastly improved quality of life.

This means taking responsibility for every penny you spend. In complete contrast to life in the debt trap, where we bury our head in the sand in the hope of avoiding the horror of our financial situation, you are going to begin a process that will make you aware of everything you spend.

Get yourself a small pocket notebook and a pen. Take them with you everywhere you go. Starting from today, every time you spend money on anything at all, write it down in the notebook. Write down what you buy and how much it costs, to the penny. If you find it easier to use a mobile phone or another hand-held device to record these details, that's fine. Your list might look something like this:

Train fare	£11.10
Coffee	£3.00
Newspaper	£1.00
Notebook and pen	£3.49

Lunch	£4.13
TOTAL	£22.72

Do this every day. It's vital that you record absolutely everything and that you record it to the last penny. Don't round the prices up or down. You need an absolutely precise account of everything you spend. Record the details as soon as possible after spending the money, so that nothing slips your mind.

Once you've got into the routine of recording your daily spending, you can start building the bigger picture.

Starting on the 1st of next month, collate your daily records every seven days and record your totals on a weekly spending sheet. Arrange the categories according to what you've paid for. They need to be detailed enough for you to get a picture of where your money is going, but not so detailed as to leave you with too many categories. For example, train and bus fares can be grouped under 'Public Transport' and the notebook and pen can go under 'Stationery'.

At the same time, if you buy a range of goods at a supermarket, e.g. food, toiletries and household cleaning products, rather than listing these items collectively under 'Supermarket' on your spending record, try to separate them.

Public Transport	£52.50
Drinks and snacks	£12.00
Groceries	£120.10

Toiletries	£18.50
Household goods	£32.45
Newspapers	£4.00
Stationery	£3.49
Fast food and snacks	£80.00
Clothes	£35.00
Cinema	£8.00
Restaurants	£50.00
Birthday present	£15.99
TOTAL	**£432.03**

At the end of the month, collate your weekly sheets into one monthly sheet. Remember to incorporate the extra days beyond the 28th. Into this monthly sheet you need to add your regular monthly outgoings: fuel bills, telephone, water, interest payments on loans, rent, mortgage payments, etc.

Now you are beginning to get a good idea of where your money goes, and from that you can build a picture of how you live your life.

Perhaps you think you don't need a financial record to tell you how you live your life. After all, it's your life and you know very well what you get up to between waking up in the morning and going to sleep at night.

Perhaps, but creating this overview of our lives for these periods often throws up some surprising facts. This is where your category headings play an important part.

The more careful you are in defining your categories, the

more focused a picture they will give you of the way you live.

For example, if you list everything you spend on food under the heading 'food', you're not giving yourself nearly as accurate a picture as if you break it down into, say, 'fast food and snacks', 'restaurants' and 'groceries'. Say your monthly food expenditure comes to £250. You might assume that £250 per month is what it costs to keep you fed for a month. But break it down and a different picture emerges. Say it shows 'fast food and snacks: £80', 'restaurants: £50' and 'groceries: £120'. Now you can begin to see the balance of your life, and identify potential areas for improvement.

£80 on fast food and snacks suggests that you're not eating as healthily as you could be. It also shows that you're wasting money, as filling up on junk food is not an economical way to eat.

The £50 spend on restaurants shows that, despite being in debt, you're still willing to pay a premium for the luxury of eating out. Obviously it's far cheaper to buy your own groceries and prepare your meals yourself. Now, I'm not saying that you should deprive yourself of life's pleasures. Remember, the whole object of this book is to enable you to lead a happy life. If you can manage to treat yourself to eating out occasionally without going further into debt and you can enjoy the experience without feeling guilty, then by all means go for it. But if the expense makes you worry then you won't enjoy it, you'll feel guilty afterwards and it will not make you happy.

The slavery of debt has many detrimental effects on our quality of life, one of which is that we don't take the trouble to look after ourselves physically, including what we eat. Another is that we deny ourselves many of life's pleasures in our attempts to cut back on spending.

The result of both these forms of self-denial is that we become physically and mentally run down, leading to deeper depression and diminished motivation to do anything about the problem.

By defining your categories in detail, you can instantly see that you need to reduce your spending on junk food and use that money to buy more healthy groceries. You will benefit financially, nutritionally and emotionally.

SEEING IS BELIEVING

In addition to painting a picture of your lifestyle, this account of your spending serves another vital purpose: it enables you to see without doubt or argument that you have a problem that needs addressing.

By the simple process of recording the words and numbers, you have overcome the fear and denial that formerly made you resist facing up to the reality of your problem. You may even find that the problem is not as serious as you had imagined. This is not uncommon. Denial doesn't always mean thinking things are better than they really are; it can often mean fearing things are worse.

AS LONG AS YOU REMAIN IN DENIAL, YOU WILL NEVER KNOW WHETHER YOUR SITUATION IS BETTER OR WORSE THAN YOU THINK. AND WITHOUT KNOWING THAT, YOU CANNOT RECTIFY IT

If you remain in denial, you will not be able to resolve your problems. By drawing up your spending log, you are replacing denial with understanding. **ONLY ONCE YOU'VE DETERMINED THE EXTENT OF YOUR DEBT CAN YOU PUT IN PLACE A STRATEGY TO CLEAR IT.**

Your spending log is a powerful tool. Armed with this record, you can now begin to lay the plans that will eradicate your debts once and for all.

With an addiction like smoking or alcoholism, it's easy to see what you need to do to quit. You stop smoking or drinking. With spending and debt, the solution is not so clear-cut. Usually there isn't only one thing you spend your money on that lands you in debt unnecessarily, there are a number of things. The key lies in identifying what those things are.

This is where the record of everything you spend comes into its own. It gets the problem out of your head and on to paper, and the result of this can be quite startling as your mental perception of the situation can be grossly inaccurate. You may exaggerate the problem in your mind, or you may underestimate it.

Very few people have the mental capacity to focus on more than a handful of things in their mind and to keep an accurate assessment of their scale and order of importance. But write them down and it suddenly becomes easy.

So it's worth taking some time to study your spending log and familiarize yourself with the fine detail. If you want to get your finances under control, you need to be totally honest with yourself about your current situation.

LEAVE NOTHING OUT

If you felt unwell and went to the doctor in the hope of being given a remedy, you would be expected to answer several questions about the symptoms of the illness, your lifestyle, what you've done in the past few weeks, etc. In order to identify the cause of your illness and prescribe a cure, the doctor will need to piece together an accurate picture of your current health. If you withheld some vital piece of information – say you'd been drinking heavily of late, or you'd been on holiday to some tropical destination – the chances are you would end up with a wrong diagnosis.

The same applies to your finances. In order to identify the cure, you need to know everything about the ailment. You need to face reality. There's nothing to fear. On the contrary, there's a marvellous new life to enjoy, free from the misery of debt.

Once you get into the swing of keeping an accurate record of your spending, you will also see exactly what you are achieving.

NO NEW DEBTS

Earlier I asked you to make a list of all the debts you'd incurred in the past year. Now take that list and hold it next to your spending log for the month. What the comparison should show, if you have followed all my instructions, is that you have arrested the trend into debt.

'But my debts haven't gone away. I still owe a fortune. And I really don't know how long I can keep going without incurring any new debts.'

I assure you your debts will go away, so there's no need to

worry about them. It may take a while but every day you go without incurring new debts is a day towards paying off ALL your debts. In other words, you are heading in the right direction. Not long ago you were heading further and further into debt. One thing was guaranteed: you were never going to pay off your debts living like that.

The simple fact is you cannot get out of debt by incurring new debts. So the most important decision you had to make was to avoid any new debts. You have done that. Perhaps you fear that you won't be able to keep it up, that sooner or later the essentials in your life will demand that you find some more money from somewhere to pay for them.

I repeat my instruction to keep an open mind, remain positive and excited about the steps you are taking towards your new life free from debt, and continue to follow all the instructions.

I mentioned that your monthly spending log is a vital tool in your fight against your debt problem. We are now going to put that tool to use.

DO THE FIGURES ADD UP?

Add up all the outgoings on your monthly spending log and write the figure down. Now write down your total income for the month, after deductions for tax, etc. Make sure you include every source of income that you have. If you are in a salaried job, this will be more straightforward than if you're self-employed.

If your monthly income varies at all throughout the year, look back at your income for the past twelve months and take a monthly average by adding it all up together and dividing the total by 12.

Now write this figure down below your total monthly outgoings. Subtract your income from your outgoings and write the figure down underneath. Like this:

Monthly outgoings

– Monthly income

= **Monthly deficit**

I'm assuming that your income is smaller than your outgoings since you have got into debt. By subtracting the former from the latter you will be left with the sum of your monthly deficit; the amount by which you lose money each month. So write a 'minus' sign in front of this figure.

Our aim is to turn that minus into a plus. There are two ways to do that: one is to increase your income – in time you will find this happening but it's not something you can be expected to do overnight. The other way is to reduce your outgoings.

We will look at ways of doing that in the next chapter. First you need to get real about where your money is going and make some clear decisions about what really matters to you in life.

PUTTING YOUR AFFAIRS IN ORDER

Your monthly spending log should currently comprise two columns: a 'category' column and a 'spend' column. You are now going to expand this into something even more instructive – a financial plan. This plan will be the route map to guide you out of debt.

You can do this on a computer or write it down manually, it's up to you. This plan is tailored to you and you alone. I cannot tell you how to spend your money, nor can anyone else. It depends on your judgement and your preferences. What I can do is show you how to make your judgements in a way that will help you to take control of your finances and hence your life.

Whichever way you choose to create this plan, make sure it's neat and legible and will not get damaged or lost. The plan will change as time passes, but you need to refer to it just as you would a map, so make sure it's kept in good order.

Create a new sheet that looks like your monthly spending log, but after the 'spend' column, add two more columns. Head them 'plan' and '+/-' respectively. Now it's time for you to start putting your outgoings in order of priority.

Starting with the Three Essentials that I set out in Chapter 11, fill in the category column. As you'll remember, the Three Essentials are Food, Warmth and Shelter, so put everything that fits those definitions down on your financial plan. You should also include your minimum payments on loans, as these are not expenses that you have any choice over. Don't fill in the actual amounts spent monthly for now, just the categories themselves. It should look something like this.

Essentials	Spend	Plan	+/-
Rent/Mortgage			
Gas & Electricity			

Water			
Council Tax			
Interest on loans			
Clothes			
Groceries			

Remember, it's important to break your food category into specific types, namely Groceries, Fast Food and Snacks, and Restaurants. Now ask yourself which of these three can be deemed essential. Perhaps you believe your spending on Fast Food and Snacks is essential to keep you nourished during the working day. If that's the case, include it in your list of essentials on the plan. In time you may want to revise this decision, but for now, it's important that the plan reflects your thinking and nobody else's.

Once you've completed your list of essentials, start transferring the figures from your monthly spending log into the 'plan' column. Why not the 'spend' column? Because we're going to use that to record your next month's spend. Your present task is to use the figures from the first month's log to make a financial plan that will guide you going forward.

Most of the essentials will remain the same from month to month, in which case simply copy the figure from the monthly log into the 'plan' column on the financial plan. However, with items like clothes, you may feel that the first month's spend was higher or lower than you are likely to spend on average. So adjust the figure to what you think is realistic and enter it in the 'plan' column.

You can round these figures up or down to the nearest pound. Unlike your daily spending log, rounding the monthly figures will make a negligible difference over time.

Once you've entered a 'plan' figure for all the essentials, draw a line under them, leaving one blank row above the line. Now start filling in the remaining categories below the line. These are your non-essential outgoings; in other words, the things that you could live without. That is not to say you should live without them. Not at all. I'm talking literally. If you had to make do without any of the items in these categories, you would not die.

We can deduce that these are all things you choose to buy because you believe that they improve your quality of life. What you need to do now is rank them in order of importance. Transfer all the non-essential categories from your monthly spending log and arrange them in order of priority, from those dearest to you to those you hold to be least important. Again, don't enter the figures from the monthly log, just the categories. Like this:

Essentials	Spend	Plan	+/−
Rent/Mortgage			
Gas & Electricity			
Water			
Council Tax			
Interest on loans			
Clothes			
Groceries			

Non-essentials	Spend	Plan	+/−
Category A			
Category B			
Category C			
Category D			
Etc			

I could give you an example of how my list would look, but we're not talking about me, we're talking about you, and your priorities will be different from mine. You don't have to spend too much time agonizing over your order of priorities. Some may change from month to month. Just try to get them in a rough order of preference.

SO HERE'S THE PLAN

Your financial plan is taking shape. You can now see before your eyes what is essential for your survival, what is important to you personally and what is not so important. Now you can fill in the remaining figures. What follows is a very methodical process that I will take you through step by step.

STEP 1

As you did with the essentials, write a figure for each non-essential category in the 'plan' column, using your monthly spending log as a guide. In each case, think about the figure you spent in the first month and ask yourself whether you're likely to spend more or less next month. For example, if you spent money on a new winter coat or new shoes in the first month, you're likely to need to spend less on clothes in an average month. Go through each category, adjusting your figures accordingly.

STEP 2

Now add up all the amounts you wrote in the essentials section and write down the total. The figure you obtain is instructive:

IT IS THE SMALLEST QUANTITY OF MONEY YOU NEED PER MONTH TO SURVIVE AS THINGS STAND

This figure needs to be lower than your monthly income. If it's not, then something has to change. Either you need to earn more money or you need to find a way to reduce your essential outgoings.

From the list of essentials, it's easy to see where the problems lie, because the list is small. You will know which of the categories could be reduced. You cannot get out of debt if your spending on essentials is greater than your income. It may mean taking a difficult decision, such as taking in a lodger or finding somewhere else to live, but surely that's preferable to continuing to haemorrhage money and careering further and further into debt?

If your income is greater than the sum of your essential outgoings, the difference is the amount you have left to spend on non-essentials. Write this figure down separately.

STEP 3

Now add up the figures you wrote in your plan column for non-essentials and deduct it from the figure you just wrote down. If you get a minus figure, then you need to reduce your planned spending on non-essentials. I will talk more about this in the next chapter.

THE FOURTH ESSENTIAL

STEP 4

I asked you to leave a blank space above the line you drew under essentials. I now want you to write 'Debt Repayment' in this space in the category column.

Remember, this plan is your route map out of debt. It's time to start clearing those debts. To begin with, just £1 in the 'plan' column will do. But unlike the figures below the line, it's not negotiable. Whatever you write down in your plan for 'Debt Repayment', you must pay it. This is my eighth instruction.

EIGHTH INSTRUCTION:
MAKE DEBT REPAYMENT YOUR FOURTH ESSENTIAL

ROBBING PETER TO PAY PAUL

As I mentioned earlier, it's not so uncommon for people with money worries to have funds tucked away in a savings or investment account. Despite the pressure they're suffering because of their mounting debts, they refuse to touch this money. They have ring-fenced it for retirement or 'a rainy day' and they don't regard it as part of their regular finances, but something sacred.

*OUT OF FEAR OF BEING DESTITUTE IN THEIR OLD
AGE, OR PERHAPS AT SOME POINT BEFORE THAT,
THEY ARE ENSURING THAT THEY ARE SUFFERING
THE MISERY OF BEING DESTITUTE NOW!*

Benjamin Franklin said, 'Creditors have better memories than debtors.' They also have higher interest rates. Bear this in mind when you come to adjust the figures in your financial plan.

*IF YOU HAVE SAVINGS, CHECK WHAT INTEREST RATE
YOU'RE GETTING. IT'S ALMOST GUARANTEED THAT
IT WON'T BE AS MUCH AS YOU'RE BEING CHARGED
BY THE LOAN COMPANIES YOU'RE INDEBTED TO*

It's understandable to like the idea of having money tucked away for emergencies, but it makes no sense to borrow at a high interest rate while investing in an account with a lower one. That's simply throwing money away. So if you are in this position, then use your savings to pay off your debts. You have now put in place the first basic steps that will bring order to your financial affairs and lead you out of debt. There is nothing to be afraid of. On the contrary, you have begun a process that will improve your quality of life and set you free from the misery and slavery of debt.

YOU DESERVE TO FEEL GOOD ABOUT THAT!

SUMMARY

- Being in control of your finances means knowing every detail. Keep your records in good order.

- Be totally honest and accurate about what you spend.

- Plan to spend your money only on things that make you genuinely happy.

- Make debt repayment your Fourth Essential.

Chapter 16

REDUCE YOUR SPENDING THE EASY WAY

IN THIS CHAPTER
•DEBT v DEBT PROBLEM •A PLAN THAT WORKS
•SELLING THE FAMILY SILVER •NON-ESSENTIALS
•BUYING FOOD AND CLOTHING

In order to balance the books, you need to reduce your spending on non-essentials. Begin by reminding yourself that these are all things you can live without.

If you have followed all the instructions, you will already have established the foundations essential for your permanent freedom from debt. In particular, you will have stopped incurring new debts.

You have done this by understanding and accepting that you have a choice over the money you spend. You have understood that there are only three essentials for survival: food, warmth and shelter. Beyond the money you spend on these three essentials you could spend nothing at all and still survive.

Maybe you think that sounds ridiculous. But millions of people on this planet do just that, and they are by no means deprived of happiness. In fact, most of them are probably considerably happier than anyone who is suffering the misery of the debt trap.

Please don't get me wrong, I'm not in any way advocating that you content yourself with living in a hut in the middle of the Amazon rainforest.

I'm just making the point that there are people who are perfectly content with such a lifestyle. There are also plenty of people who have dropped out of Western society to seek happiness in a life with no possessions. It may not be the life for you, but it shows that material possessions are not essential for human happiness.

IN FACT, THE DESIRE FOR MATERIAL POSSESSIONS IS OFTEN THE CAUSE OF MISERY

We are now going to focus on the things you choose to buy purely out of desire: the non-essentials.

You have reached the turning point in your debt problem and are ready to begin your progress out of debt. It hasn't been a painful struggle and no physical effort has been required. The fears you had of confronting your problem were the result of illusions, which have now been removed. You now realise there is nothing to fear. All you had to do was choose a new direction. It was as easy as that.

SUCCESS!

At the beginning of this book I claimed that you will be able to continue to buy everything you need and lead a rich and fulfilling life, while clearing all your debts, removing all your money worries and rebuilding your relationships, making you happier than you can imagine.

Perhaps you think you still have a huge distance to go before you can be in that happy position, because you still have a debt problem. Not so. You still have debts but you no longer have a problem.

The problem was your inability to confront the situation and put in place a fail-safe plan to resolve it. In particular you needed to avoid going further into debt by continuing to buy things you don't need and which do not make you happy. Now you've reversed that situation, and you've done it by reversing the brainwashing that has kept you in the debt trap.

You have every reason to feel elated. Your debt problem is effectively over.

'But what about the money I still owe in loans?'

Why is that a problem? Because it needs to be paid off? No problem, you can pay it off. There's no need to be afraid of it. There are millions of people in exactly the same boat and they don't go through life suffering the fear and humiliation that you have suffered. They don't consider themselves to have a problem at all. They're called mortgage holders.

They have hundreds of thousands of pounds of debt, but they don't see it as a reason to panic. Why? Because they have an agreed plan with the mortgage lender for paying it off.

It follows that all you need in order to get rid of your debt problem is a plan. And now you have one: the financial plan that you drew up in the last chapter.

A PLAN THAT WORKS

We still have some work to do on your financial plan. You have established your essentials and the amount you plan to spend on them in the coming month. You have also established your non-essentials in order of priority, and the amount you plan to spend on each of them. Assuming the total is in excess of your monthly income, it will be impossible to follow this plan without going further into debt. We agreed that there are two ways to balance the books: one is to increase your income, the other is to reduce your non-essential outgoings.

The latter option offers the most immediate scope, with one exception.

SELLING THE FAMILY SILVER

Selling your possessions is a tempting way to bring in extra income. There's nothing wrong with selling things you no longer need or want and people in debt often have plenty of those as they have a tendency to spend money on junk in an attempt to cheer themselves up. But selling things to balance the books in the short term is not a plan for life. After all, you can only sell something once. It's not a regular source of income and, therefore, it should not be used as part of your financial plan.

It can also lead to misery. You may begin by selling things you no longer need or want, but if you come to rely on it as a way of making ends meet, you will inevitably end up selling things of significant personal value. What's more, you will not be addressing the most important issue, and that is to rearrange your finances so that they balance in the long term, month after month.

REARRANGING YOUR SPENDING

So how can you reduce your spending on non-essentials without committing yourself to a life of misery?

When you look at your financial plan and the figures you've put by each category for the next month, you may be able to find a way to justify every penny. But remember, these are non-essentials. You could carry on living without any of them. The only real reason you have for any of that spending is that it's money you choose to spend.

And as long as you choose to spend your money on non-essentials, there are plenty of people who will be only too happy to take it from you. At the same time they will try to con you that the items involved are essential and make you feel that you're getting value for money because they want you to keep coming back for more.

An irony of the way many people in debt prioritize their spending is that one of the first things they tend to cut out is personal pleasure. I'm talking about genuine treats, such as a meal in a restaurant, a film, a show or taking a holiday. Instead they seek comfort in junk-spending on smaller things, each of which they consider to be insignificant in its impact on their finances, but when taken together add up to a large part of their non-essential spending.

You can make a significant impact on your non-essential spending by stopping junk-spending. Watch out for false economies, so-called bargains that entice you into buying twice as much as you want and serve only to make you spend and consume more. Ignore special offers unless it's something that you genuinely want and always stop to think instead of making impulse purchases.

Remember, every penny you spend is a penny more to earn. Think of each item in terms of the number of hours you'll have to work to earn that amount of money. Ask yourself, 'Does this fall within my financial plan? Do I really need it?' If you do need it but it falls outside your plan, do you have to have it now? Can't it wait until you do have the money? After all, these are non-essentials we're talking about here. All of it can wait. And if you do wait, you may well find that by the time you have the money, you don't really need or want it any more.

An effective way to make you think twice about your non-essential spending is to match it with savings. For every penny you spend on a non-essential, put the same amount into a savings account. Think you can't afford to do both? Which would be more beneficial to you right now?

FOOD FOR THOUGHT

The process of reducing your non-essential spending is a gradual one. It's highly unlikely in your first month that you will spend exactly what you planned to in each category. Some will be higher than you planned, others will be lower. Over time you will be able to judge your planned spending more accurately.

It also requires some significant changes in the way you go about your life. To this end, it's instructive to start by focusing on two categories that fall into both your essentials and your non-essentials: food and clothing.

As I've mentioned, a lot of the food we buy is non-essential. It is of negligible nutritional value and we could certainly live without it. However, we obviously need a regular supply of food to survive. To begin with, I want you to try an experiment. I'm not going to ask you to change your dietary habits, rather I want you to think about where your food comes from. For the next week, I want you to buy all your food either from street markets (where it can be extremely good value), from the grocer's, butcher's or fishmonger's or from the supermarket and nothing from fast food outlets, snack bars or sweetshops.

If you usually buy a sandwich for lunch, buy the ingredients instead and make it yourself before you leave home in the morning. Instead of grabbing a burger on the way home, make time to prepare a nutritious meal for yourself and eat it at the table.

Try to eat plenty of fresh fruit and vegetables. They are both cheap and nutritious. If you like a snack during the day at work, take some fruit or a bag of nuts with you. The key here is to plan ahead.

THE RESULT WILL BE AN INCREASE IN YOUR GROCERY BILL, BUT A ZERO IN THE SPEND COLUMN FOR FAST FOOD AND SNACKS

The money you save on non-essential food will be more than the extra you spend on groceries and you will feel better, look better and have much more energy because you will be eating more healthily.

Continue this experiment and the likelihood is that it will soon become your normal lifestyle because you will enjoy the benefits. You will become better at economizing on ingredients, making the food you buy go further and cutting out waste. This adjustment will make you happier and healthier and could reduce your spending on food by a significant amount.

DRESS TO IMPRESS

Clothing is another category that lies in both essential and non-essential spending. We need clothes to keep warm and we're required by law to wear clothes in public. Some spending on clothing is, therefore, essential. But are all the clothes you buy absolutely essential?

Don't you choose most of them on the basis of style rather than practicality? Being comfortable with your appearance is an important part of happiness, but there is a judgement to be made here between clothes you need and clothes you don't need.

Only you can make that judgement and it's important that you do. If clothes are particularly important to your happiness, then it makes sense for you to allocate more of your financial plan to buying clothes than someone to whom they are unimportant. But if you buy clothes to try to keep up with fashion, then you leave yourself open to junk-spending.

There is a significant parallel between buying clothes and buying food. That parallel is 'quality'. Nutritious food is actually more economical than junk food because it genuinely satisfies your hunger by giving your body the nutrients it needs, so you don't have to keep stuffing yourself with junk. Plus it makes you feel healthier and look fitter.

With clothes, spending a little extra on something that is well made will save you money in the long run, rather than spending regular small amounts on cheap clothing that is not made to last, doesn't fit you as comfortably and doesn't look as good.

Try applying this principle to all your non-essential spending. Cheap products are easier to buy; so easy that they are given little thought. When you've got large debts, it's hard to see how a few pounds can make a difference. But a few pounds here and there quickly adds up, especially if the things you buy are quickly used up and discarded, and need replacing on a regular basis.

LITTLE MONSTERS

People's financial plans often include large sums of money for cigarettes, alcohol and other drugs. When you ask them why they're taking money from other categories to spend on these, they either reply, 'They are essential' or 'You said I shouldn't sacrifice my pleasures in life'.

All addictions are based on illusions. Addicts regard the cigarette, the drink or whatever as a pleasure and a crutch and fear that they won't be able to enjoy life or handle stress without it. It doesn't occur to them that they didn't need it before they started taking it and that people who don't take it are perfectly capable of enjoying life to the full and coping with adversity.

Nor does it occur to them that non-addicts do not get that feeling of 'needing a fix' at regular intervals to prevent them from getting uptight. This is because all drug addictions work back to front. It's not when you take the drug that you experience the withdrawal. On the contrary, you get uptight from the withdrawal between fixes and when you take the drug it seems to relieve the insecure feeling and so you feel more relaxed.

The drug, therefore, gets the credit for relieving the withdrawal but not the blame for causing it in the first place. Hence the illusion of a pleasure and a crutch.

Money spent on these addictions is not just wasted, it's spent on something which gives you no genuine pleasure or crutch and causes you terrible harm. Quite apart from the diseases, the slavery and the social stigma, the average 20-a-day smoker spends around £100,000 in their lifetime on cigarettes. As you begin the process of rearranging your finances to create a workable plan for a life without debt, one of the greatest things you can do for yourself is to get free from any other addictions you are suffering, as that will immediately and significantly decrease your spending and simultaneously radically improve the quality of your life.

If you're a smoker, I can imagine you're thinking, 'Oh my God! He's telling me I've got to quit!' No, I'm not. Only you can decide when and how to stop. However, it is true that the longer you pour money into your addiction, the longer it will take you to clear your debts. If you're a smoker, or you have problems with alcohol, other drugs or over-eating, I recommend reading my books on those subjects or attending one of our clinics, where we guarantee you will quit or your money back. Details of our clinics can be found at the back of this book.

> ## MAKE IT REAL
>
> In order to keep an accurate eye on your non-essential spending, use cash as much as possible. You know what your budget is. Make one cash withdrawal per week and tell yourself that when the money's gone, it's gone. This will help you to follow your Financial Plan and keep within your spending limit.

REVISE YOUR PLAN

Once you've accepted that the items in your non-essentials category really are things you can live without, go through your financial plan again and revise your planned spending figures under non-essentials until your outgoings amount to less than your income.

Begin at the bottom, with your least favourite things and work your way up the list. You may well find that you balance the books before you get to your favourite categories at the top. If so, well done. Remember that our ultimate aim is your happiness. With each category, ask yourself how much happiness you derive from the money you spend.

If the answer is 'none', put a zero in that column and save your money for something more valuable to you.

SUMMARY

- Material possessions are not essential for human happiness.

- Having a debt is not the same as having a debt problem.

- Be wary of selling possessions in order to balance the books in the short term.

- Think carefully about all your purchases, large and small, and beware of false economies.

- Think seriously about your smoking, drinking, eating and/or other drug consumption. If you're ready to address these, go for it with Allen Carr's Easyway method.

- Revise your financial plan so that your outgoings amount to less than your income.

Chapter 17

TREATING YOURSELF

IN THIS CHAPTER
•*YOU DON'T NEED TO SUFFER* •*LESS IS MORE*
•*OUT WITH THE OLD* •*A WISH LIST*
•*TREATING NOT SPOILING* •*GIVING IS GREAT*

Invest in your own personal happiness and getting out of debt will feel even easier.

When you're struggling to get out of debt, the idea of spending money on personal indulgences seems out of the question. The first thing many people sacrifice when they try to cut their spending is personal pleasure.

The trouble is that we've actually been brainwashed into thinking that getting out of debt needs to be a terrible struggle involving deprivation and sacrifice.

Society comes down hard on people in debt. They receive little sympathy. The general feeling is that they've been irresponsible by over-indulging themselves and have no one else to blame. Now that they're in debt, the good times have to stop and they have to endure a period of hardship to get back into the black.

Sadly, this attitude rubs off on people in debt themselves. The pressure and anxiety puts us in a miserable state of mind and we feel guilty, ashamed and lacking in self-worth. We end up believing that we deserve a gruelling period of self-sacrifice.

In fact, that's exactly what you don't need. You may still find this difficult to believe, but the fact is you can actually enjoy the process of becoming debt-free.

First it's essential to dispel any feelings of doom or gloom and approach the challenge with a growing sense of positivity and excitement. Remember my third instruction: **BEGIN WITH A FEELING OF ELATION**.

You can't do that if you're forever feeling deprived of the things that truly make you happy. Happiness is the main objective here. If you were happy despite your debts, it wouldn't be a problem. But the reason you're reading this book is because your debts have made you miserable.

When you're in a miserable frame of mind, it's hard to see anything in a positive light. It blunts your creativity. Where there are possibilities and opportunities, you see only hazards and obstacles. Instead of focusing on the reasons for doing things, you focus on the reasons not to.

In order to put into effect a working plan for getting out of debt, you need to see the possibilities in that plan and be clear in your mind that it will work. If instead you chose to focus on the possible reasons why it might not work, you would be courting failure. But you don't even have to think about failure if you follow the instructions, because success will be inevitable.

So dismiss the belief that you need to suffer in order to succeed. The opposite is the case.

THE MARK OF SUCCESS IS THE VERY FACT THAT YOU ARE NOT SUFFERING ANY MORE AND HAVE STOPPED PUNISHING YOURSELF

So let's concentrate on putting the genuine pleasures back into your life.

LESS IS MORE

Here's another principle that many people often find hard to grasp:

THE FIRST PART OF THE PROCESS OF GETTING WHAT YOU WANT IS GETTING RID OF WHAT YOU DON'T WANT

People in debt are often so obsessed with acquiring things, the idea of getting rid of them is anathema to them. It seems to go against logic. 'I'm trying to increase my assets, not reduce them.'

But accumulating assets is not the objective. If you focus on that you make yourself a slave to money and put yourself back in the trap. As a result of following this method, you may well become wealthy but the objective is not wealth, it's happiness. Happiness is not about having lots of possessions, it's about having the possessions you want.

Let's follow the William Morris principle. Look around your house, take every object in turn and ask yourself whether you know it to be useful or believe it to be beautiful. I find that a good place to start is my sock drawer. A new pair of comfortable socks is a small thing that gives great pleasure. By the same token, an old pair with holes in the toes or heel is a great annoyance. If you have socks like that, throw them out now.

Do the same with all your clothes. Wearing clothes that don't fit you comfortably or make you look shabby can put you in a bad mood all day. Why torture yourself? Get rid of them.

Once you've sorted through all your clothes, move on to another area, such as the kitchen. Do you have utensils that you never use? Chances are they're obstructing your access to the things you do use. Be ruthless. Few kitchen utensils are beautiful, and if they're of no use to you, get rid of them. Put them in a pile on your living room floor.

Continue going through your home, weeding out everything that is superfluous and putting it in the same pile. By the time you've finished, you may have a quite substantial pile of possessions on your living room floor. More significantly, you will have created space amongst the things you've decided to keep.

I compare this process to nurturing a fruit tree. In order to achieve a healthy crop of fruit, there are two things you need to do that involve reducing the tree. The first is to prune it. This involves not only cutting off the dead wood but also cutting back perfectly healthy shoots, which, to the uninitiated seems counterproductive. However, this serves to focus the strength of the tree into the growing tips, which increases the amount of fruit.

The second part of the process is to cull the fruit. Each growing point will produce a cluster of fruits, not all of which can make it to maturity. If all are left on the tree, the size and health of the fruit will be hampered. Nature causes the smaller, weaker fruits to drop off, but for a really healthy crop it's best to reduce each cluster to just one fruit.

Again, this seems counterproductive when you see all those budding fruits in spring, but come harvest time the results justify the action. The strongest buds have been given the space and nourishment to grow into healthy, mature fruit.

The same principle applies to your possessions. In order to get the most out of the ones you really want, you need to get rid of the ones you don't.

This requires a certain amount of confidence, especially in the case of clothes. For example, we tend to hang on to old socks because we don't have new ones to replace them. Throw out the old ones and we won't have any socks at all, right? Try it and see what happens.

If, by throwing out all your annoying old worn-out socks, you find yourself short, you'll make it a priority to buy yourself new ones. When you put them on you'll wonder why you didn't do it ages ago, rather than forcing yourself to go on suffering with the old ones.

Simply by getting rid of something that gives you no pleasure, you have brought about its replacement with something that does. That's what happens when you take the time to evaluate what's really important to you. Perhaps you think it sounds like some kind of magic. It's not. It's just your subconscious mind being allowed to have its say.

MAKE A WISH LIST

Despite the delusions and misery of being in debt, your subconscious mind always recognised the things that would make you truly happy. That's why you were miserable: there was a clash between your true feelings and the choices you were making. Those choices were being manipulated by brainwashing.

Now we're going to let your true feelings come to the fore. I want you to write down all the things that you really want in life. Forget what's realistic and what's not, this is your chance to express your dreams.

Start with the heading 'Lifestyle'. Beneath this heading, write down a description of how you would like your day-to-day life to be, the things you would like to own, the place you would like to live, etc. Be completely open and free. If there's something you've always wanted, write it down.

Now do the same under the heading 'Relationships'. How much time would you like to spend with friends and family? Who are the people that matter most to you? Is there someone you want to share your life with, or if you already do, are there improvements you could make to the time you spend together? Write it all down. This is for your eyes only.

Continue your wish list with the following headings:

Money

Work

Leisure

Creativity

Self-improvement

I repeat, let your feelings flow. Perhaps you've always wanted to own a yacht but you consider this way beyond your means. Write it down. There is nothing unrealistic about owning a yacht. There are thousands of yacht owners in the world. Why shouldn't you be one of them? You might not achieve it today, or even next year, but if you tell yourself it's never going to happen, all you do is ensure that it won't.

Once you've written your wish list, read it through. This will give you a picture of your ideal life and serve as a useful guide in making decisions in relation to your financial plan. Choosing how to allocate your money to the different categories among your non-essentials will become easier, because your awareness of what you really want, what makes you truly happy, will take the place of the misinformation that misguided you while you were in the debt trap.

You can add to this guide with other wish lists. For example:

10 things I want to see before I die

10 skills I want to learn

10 things I want to own

TREATING NOT SPOILING

Focusing on the things you would like to do will put you in a positive, upbeat frame of mind. Remember, 'less is more'. Prioritizing time and money for treating yourself to the real pleasures in life is not the same as trying to feel better by junk-spending all the time. One is selective and highly rewarding, the other is thoughtless and highly damaging.

You want your life to be like a fruit tree, in which every fruit is healthy and fully formed. If you confuse treating yourself to valuable experiences with lavishing meaningless gifts on yourself, your tree will be overburdened and the fruits withered and bitter.

GETTING RID OF THE JUNK

So you have a pile of possessions on your living room floor. How are you going to get rid of them?

You have three choices:

1. Throw them in the bin
2. Sell them
3. Give them away.

With a number of items – your old socks, for example – there is only one choice. So throw them in the bin.

Now look at what you're left with. You may not have any use for it but it could be useful to someone. So what do you do? Sell it?

These days, it's very easy to sell just about anything that you no longer have a use for. It's incredible what people will pay money for on eBay!

Any money you can raise by selling these items could be useful, but remember, I strongly advise against adding it to your financial plan. You could use it to treat yourself to a meal out or whatever, or you could use it to pay off some of your debts.

But consider option 3 – giving it away. Let's face it, you're already profiting by getting rid of this stuff. Now you have an opportunity to gain something extra from it: the pleasure of giving.

Again, the idea of giving seems counterintuitive if you believe that your problem requires you to hold on to as much as you can. In fact, giving can be hugely beneficial to you as you make your way out of debt.

OK, you will not get any direct financial return, but you will do something to your state of mind that you will find quite startling. You will feel a sense of control.

I recommend that you add 'Giving' as a category in your financial plan. Even if it's just £1 a month to charity, the very fact that you are putting yourself in a position to give marks a complete turnaround in your situation.

While in the debt trap, you were a slave to money. You had no control over it. As a giver, you are making a financial choice that shows you're in control.

In addition to that, you will feel good about yourself, something you were unable to feel before.

GIVING SHOULD BE SEEN AS ANOTHER WAY OF TREATING YOURSELF, BECAUSE YOU ARE USING YOUR MONEY TO GIVE YOURSELF GENUINE PLEASURE.

SUMMARY

- Dispel any feelings of doom or gloom.
- Misery blunts your creativity and blinds you to opportunities.
- If you focus on wealth you will become a slave to money.
- To get what you want, get rid of what you don't want.
- Be positive about your desires. Tell yourself something won't happen and you merely guarantee that it won't.
- Make giving part of your plan – it reinforces your sense of financial control and makes you feel good about yourself.

Chapter 18

THE FOURTH ESSENTIAL

IN THIS CHAPTER

• THE WITHDRAWAL PERIOD • YOUR OBLIGATION TO REPAY
• FACE YOUR DEBTS • SMALL ACORNS • TIPPING THE BALANCE
• INTEREST • DEALING WITH YOUR CREDITORS • RECIPE FOR HAPPINESS

Clearing your debts is part of the process of freeing yourself from the control of your creditors. Enjoy it!

> *You don't have to wait until you've cleared your debts to be free from the debt trap. The beautiful truth is that by the time you come to pay off your debts, your debt problem has already been solved.*

AFTER THE MOMENT OF REVELATION

When smokers quit by using Easyway, they experience a moment of revelation. This is the moment when they realise they no longer need or desire a cigarette. The feeling is one of ecstatic happiness. They are free from a trap that was making them miserable, ill, anti-social and costing them a fortune.

The moment of revelation usually comes soon after smoking the final cigarette. The act of smoking that cigarette marks the end of their addiction to nicotine. By the time they crush out the last burning embers, they're free from the illusions that had kept them trapped.

Your debt problem ended when you committed to not incurring any new debts. That was the turning point, the moment you escaped the debt trap and began your progress out of debt. Congratulations! You have achieved something marvellous. You no longer borrow money because you recognise and understand that you don't need to in order to lead a happy life, and that going into debt makes you miserable.

'But I'm still in debt!'

Having debts is not the same as having a debt problem. Millions of people have huge debts in the form of a mortgage. They're not miserable, stressed or scared. They simply regard their mortgage as a business transaction that stretches over a long period.

When a smoker quits, there follows a brief period of withdrawal as the body gets rid of all the nicotine and repairs itself. I'm not talking about the torture people suffer when they try to quit on the willpower method. That's psychological and entirely avoidable if you use Easyway. I'm talking about the very mild physical withdrawal that occurs over the first few days. The human body is remarkable in this respect; it restores itself in a very short time. In fact, the physical withdrawal is so slight that most people who use Easyway report that it's scarcely noticeable.

It takes longer to wipe your debt slate clean, but in principle the repayment period is similar to the smoker's physical withdrawal period. It happens after the problem has been solved. All that's required is for the person to understand the method and follow the instructions. The amount of time it takes is irrelevant because the problem has gone and you can get on with leading a happy life.

Clearing your debts is only a problem if you imagine it to be. People often panic about the size of their debt. It looks to them like a mountain, an insurmountable barrier that will forever block their path to happiness. But it's not. All debts are surmountable, provided you follow the right method.

YOUR OBLIGATION TO REPAY

I am going to take you now through a simple, methodical solution for paying off your debts. You probably think your creditors are in control. Not so. This method will see you clear your debts on your terms and you'll be in control all the way.

BUT that doesn't mean you can play fast and loose with your creditors. You've borrowed this money and you have to pay it back. Perhaps that thought annoys you. It's funny, isn't it, how we borrow money so carelessly and yet feel anger and resentment when we're asked to repay it?

That anger and resentment are caused by fear and anxiety. The fear of being unable to pay it back without terrible hardship and the anxiety of being reminded that you're going deeper and deeper into the debt trap. It's also caused by finding yourself under financial pressure because of buying things you don't value. If you felt the cost was worthwhile, your resentment would be significantly reduced. But most of the things people in debt spend their borrowed money on are of little or no value to them in the long run.

Now that you're no longer trapped, you can put aside any negative feelings about paying the money back. On the contrary, I want you to take pleasure in the thought of returning every penny, not for the sake of your creditors but for your own sake.

There's no longer any need to be evasive, secretive or dishonest. You're about to discover the joy of having nothing to hide. You're going to be up-front and honest, open, reliable and committed to paying back everything you owe. Rejoice! This is going to be one of the most enjoyable experiences you've had for a long time.

BUILD THE MOUNTAIN

In any process that requires planning and negotiation, knowledge is power. It's important that you know everything there is to know about your financial situation. As I mentioned before, many people shy away from this because they're afraid of the size of their debts. The fact is they have no idea just how big (or small) their debts are.

But that's not you. You have nothing to be afraid of. You're going to begin by facing the debt and recognizing precisely what you're dealing with. You're going to become the world's leading expert on the subject of your financial situation.

Make a list of everyone to whom you owe money. There's no need to include your mortgage, if you have one, because that's already accounted for in your financial plan. However, if you've fallen behind with your repayments, or your rent, you need to include that amount in your debt list.

Make sure you include every penny.

This list of different types of loan may help you:

• Unsecured bank loan

• Overdraft on your current account

• Credit cards and store cards

• Credit finance arrangements (e.g. car loan)

• Student loan

• Personal loans from friends and family

• Advance on your salary

• Services rendered but not yet paid for

• Defaulted rent or mortgage payments

• Tax.

Make two columns on your spreadsheet, write down every individual creditor in the left-hand column and the amount you owe them in the right. Don't include interest. You should already have that accounted for on your financial plan. What we're concerned with now is the sum borrowed. I'm told capital repayments are included in minimum credit card repayments and unsecured bank loan repayments.

BUILDING YOUR PLAN

Now take your Financial Plan. By now you should have balanced it so that the total of your outgoings is equal to or less than your income. This plan represents the route map by which you will find your way out of debt and you will soon grow accustomed to it. It will change here and there as you progress and develop a clearer picture of how you want to prioritize your spending, so you may want to work with it for a month or two before you put in a figure for the fourth essential: debt repayment. But don't leave it for longer than three months.

THIS IS A BIG PART OF THE PLEASURE OF GETTING OUT OF DEBT, SO WHY DELAY?

Start small. Remember, the size of your debt is not what matters; your ability to repay it is the guiding principle and only you can evaluate what that is. Perhaps you've found that there's a surplus in your Financial Plan, in which case you can enter this amount for Debt Repayment. However, it's more likely that you've had to squeeze the figures to make them fit and you're struggling to see where you're going to find any money for repayments.

Ask yourself a question: how important is £1 to me? Which of your non-essential outgoings would be sabotaged if you reduced planned spending by £1 or more? Perhaps you feel that some have no margin left in them. Your fares for getting to work, for example. But what if you walked or cycled at least occasionally or part of the way? How much could you save? Remember, it all adds up.

Go through all your non-essentials and reduce their planned spending by as much as you can. Now add up how much you've saved and put that figure in the box for Debt Repayment.

Now go back to your Debt Record. Add up all your debts and write the total at the bottom of the right-hand column. Now calculate each individual debt as a percentage of this total. Here's the formula:

INDIVIDUAL DEBT DIVIDED BY TOTAL DEBT, MULTIPLIED BY 100

For example, say my total debt amounts to £28,500, of which I owe £1,200 on a store card. I would calculate the store's percentage thus:

1,200 / 28,500 = 0.042

0.042 x 100 = 4.2

So the store's share of my debts would be 4.2%.

Apply this calculation to all your individual debts. If you find the mathematics confusing, get a friend who understands it to help you. Make a third column to the right of the money owed column and write the percentages in here. If you add them all up, they should come to 100.

Now make a fourth column and head it 'Repayment'. For each debt, calculate the relevant percentage of the amount you have made available for Debt Repayment on your financial plan, and write this in the Repayment column on your Debt Register.

For example, if you've made available £200 per month, you can calculate the amount you can repay to your store card like this:

200 x 4.2/100 = £8.40.

Your sheet may look something like this.

Creditor	Amount owed	% of total debt	Repayments
Car loan	£6,400	22.5%	£45.00
Bank loan	£5,000	17.5%	£35.00
Builder	£3,200	11.3%	£22.50
Credit card 1	£3,000	10.5%	£21.10
Credit card 2	£2,800	9.8%	£19.60
Overdraft	£2,500	8.8%	£17.60
Tax	£2,400	8.4%	£16.80
Loan from dad	£2,000	7.0%	£14.00
Store card	£1,200	4.2%	£8.40
TOTAL	**£28,500**	**100.0%**	**£200.00**

Please note that these figures don't include monthly interest (see essential payments, p.186-8). This table is just an example of how someone could reduce their debts – your repayments could be higher or lower depending on your circumstances.

FROM SMALL ACORNS...

If your sheet does look like this, you're probably thinking, 'At £200 a month I'm never going to pay off my £28,500 debt.' But as you continue to follow your plan, you'll find that your debt decreases faster and faster. Remember, before you got out of the debt trap you weren't paying off your debts at all; you were adding to them. The fact that you're repaying anything marks a major turnaround in the way you control your finances.

YOU ARE NOW IN CONTROL

Debt Trap   Clean Slate

Think of a seesaw. At one end is the Debt Trap, at the other end is the Clean Slate. Before you started reading this book you were standing on the Debt Trap end and so the seesaw tipped towards debt. Now you have turned round and started making your way back along the seesaw towards the Clean Slate. As you progress, the seesaw begins to rise out of debt. The further along the seesaw you go, the faster it rises, until you reach the middle. Now you've reached the tipping point. As you continue to move along, the seesaw tips faster and faster and before you know it, you've arrived at the Clean Slate.

This method works in the same way. When you start to pay off your debts, you automatically and immediately reduce your outgoings as your interest payments are reduced. This reduction is small to begin with, but the further you go, the bigger it gets. You can use the money saved in Interest Payments to increase your Debt Repayments, and so the debt is paid off at an ever-increasing rate.

It's so satisfying and enjoyable to see your debts being reduced. In your record book, make a page for each creditor and write the amount you owe them. Then write the amount of your first monthly payment underneath, subtract one from the other and write the new amount underneath. Repeat this every month for every debt and you will see that seesaw tip.

THE POWER OF FAIR PLAY

Perhaps you're wondering why I haven't told you to use your repayment budget to pay off the creditor with the highest interest rate first. After all, wouldn't this be the quickest way to reduce your total debt? Unfortunately, if you only paid off one creditor, you would still be chased by the others and your situation would barely change.

At the moment all your creditors are demanding a minimum monthly repayment, which comprises the monthly interest plus a proportion of the outstanding debt. If you fail to pay it each month, they add a charge to your account, which increases your total debt. Unless you make the minimum payment, your debt will continue to increase and your creditors will not get their money. It's a situation that suits nobody.

You are going to remedy that situation by going to your creditors with a new proposal that suits all parties by reducing your minimum payment to an amount you can afford. However, in order to achieve this you have to be able to show ALL your creditors that you have a plan to pay them back. That's why I haven't told you to allocate all your repayment budget to the one that charges the highest interest at this stage. If you did, you would have no bargaining power with your remaining creditors and would remain in the same hopeless predicament. Stick to your plan and stay in control.

As you make more money available for Debt Repayment, then you can allocate it to the creditor that's charging you the highest interest rate until that debt is paid off. Then allocate it to the next highest and so on. But keep paying your remaining creditors at the rate calculated in your initial repayment plan.

TIME TO EXERCISE YOUR CONTROL

If you are to be the leading expert on your financial situation, you not only need to know everything about the money you make and the money you owe, you also need to know all your options. The chances are you're paying some pretty exorbitant interest rates on your loans. But do you have to?

Do some research. Shop around and find out what rates other lenders are offering. There are numerous options available, many of which people fail to spot because they refuse to pay attention to their financial situation. They go on paying a higher rate just because they're too afraid to address the situation, and so keep their head in the sand.

Now that you've reversed the slide into debt, you're in a much stronger position to negotiate with your creditors. Again, this is a prospect that fills many people with dread. But not you. You are different from the person you were when you first picked up this book, in two key ways:

1. You know the facts
2. You are hiding nothing.

When you have nothing to hide, there is no fear of being caught out. You can face your creditors with confidence, knowing that you are the expert on your finances. You are not going into a conflict. You have the same objective: the repayment of your debt. It's simply a question of finding the best way to do it.

They may know how they <u>want</u> it to be done, and the more you hide from them, the more they will try to impose their will on you.

You know how it *needs* to be done, and the best way to communicate that is to come forward, present them with the facts and deliver your proposal.

Ask them for two things:

1. A reduction in your interest rate
2. A fixed minimum monthly payment that amounts to your new interest payment plus the amount you have calculated that you can pay back.

'But my creditors are going to laugh at me if I offer them £5 a month.' Maybe they will. People laughed at Columbus when he said the Earth was round. They didn't know the facts.

If £5 a month is all you can afford right now, it's not absurd, it's reality. And there's no reason to feel ashamed about it. It doesn't matter what people think, you know the facts and the fact is that £5 is all you can manage at the moment. It's as simple as that. It's also £5 more than you were paying off before. And remember, you're still paying the interest. Once they see you're serious about your plan, they will take you seriously too.

As soon as you have your Debt Repayment Plan ready, start contacting your creditors. The human touch is very powerful in this situation, so use methods that show the real person behind the debt as much as possible. Ask to come in and see them, at least for the first contact. Remember the salesman's technique and use it in your favour: when you make a proposition to someone in person, they find it harder to say no. It's easier to say no over the phone, and easier still in writing. So plan your approach accordingly.

Keep calm and draw strength from your knowledge of the subject. Remember, they will not be used to people in your situation coming to them on their own initiative. They will be surprised and, though they may not show it, impressed.

Their first reaction may well be to stick to the usual line and refuse your proposal. This is where the human touch comes into its own. Use the facts you have gathered to paint an accurate picture of your situation for them. Explain that you have had a serious debt problem and are on a programme of debt repayment. Show them how you plan to do it and explain how your repayments have been divided fairly between all your creditors.

As your arguments build up in front of them, theirs will fall away. Imagine if someone told you the Earth was round and you thought it was flat. Then they showed that if you sailed to the west and kept going, you arrived back where you started, from the east. Then they showed you a photograph of Earth taken from space. And finally they put you in a rocket and orbited the Earth so you could see it for yourself. By the end of all that you would have no choice but to accept the fact that the Earth is round.

This is the approach you need to take with your creditors. Present them with all the evidence until they have to accept that your proposal is the only viable one. If the first person you speak to refuses to see reason, it may be because they don't have the authority to go against company policy. Ask to speak to their manager, politely and calmly, until you come to somebody who does have the authority.

Keep a record of everything that passes between you and

your creditors: every meeting, every phone call, every letter and every email. Confirm any agreements you come to in writing. Be efficient and conscientious – two traits that are not normally associated with people who have debt problems. Others are:

REMORSE

From the first contact, apologise for having got into this situation. Creditors are used to aggression and resentment when negotiating repayments. By showing that you accept your predicament, that you're not trying to deny your previous financial mismanagement and that you are now serious about rectifying the situation, you will increase the chances of a sympathetic reaction.

COMMITMENT

Tell them you are committed to repaying your debt in full. Show them your financial plan as proof that you have a system in place for doing just that.

RELIABILITY

Do everything you promise to do, when you promise to do it. That way, once you've got an agreed repayment plan in place, they can't suddenly change the terms by claiming that you've failed to honour your side of the agreement. That way you remain in control.

Your aim is to build a relationship with each lender without becoming a nuisance. The more they get to understand your predicament and see how you're organizing yourself to resolve it, the more they will feel inclined to help.

If, after all this, the creditor is slow to respond to your proposal, start sending them the money anyway. Remember, you're doing things on your terms now. Just make sure you keep proof of every penny you send. Rearranging your debts can save you a lot of money over time, and any money released can be added to your Debt Repayment figure, speeding up the rate at which you wipe the slate clean.

Just beware of two potential dangerous pitfalls. You will no doubt come across numerous firms offering to restructure your debts for you. AVOID THEM! They can't offer anything that you can't do yourself and they will only add a further burden to your existing debt. Another temptation is transferring unsecured loans to secured loans. In other words, providing a guarantee for the money you borrow in the form of your house, car or other assets, in exchange for a lower rate of interest. Avoid this temptation at all costs. It's a very good way to lose your house!

A RECIPE FOR HAPPINESS

There's nothing difficult about any of this. Apart from some simple mathematics, all it requires is a little time and commitment. That's not much to ask and the benefits are fantastic. Putting it all down in writing enables you to see exactly what you're trying to do and gives you the knowledge you need to progress out of debt. It also enables you to see what you're achieving, month after month, which in turn adds to your motivation, confidence and happiness.

THE SEESAW IS TIPPING IN YOUR FAVOUR.

Knowing your finances inside out and having detailed records to hand will serve you well when negotiating with your creditors. Should they prove intransigent and resort to debt collectors or the courts, your records will provide compelling evidence in your defence.

ACCENTUATE THE POSITIVE

In order to find the money to clear your debts, we have concentrated on reducing your outgoings. Another way, as I mentioned previously, is to increase your income.

Once you have your Financial Plan, you no longer need to carry financial concerns around in your head. It's all down on record if you need to refer to it, but you know it adds up, so all you really have to do is follow it. This freedom has a truly amazing effect on your mindset. No longer obsessed with penny pinching, you begin to develop a positive, creative outlook and a happier demeanour. You begin to recognise opportunities that previously passed you by, and when you go for them, you create a favourable impression with your positive energy.

What once seemed like a forlorn hope – increasing your income – is now a very real possibility that presents itself at every turn.

The key is to take your opportunities when they come. With your confidence restored, you will feel more inclined to put yourself in for job opportunities. Moreover, your creative mindset will help you to see opportunities that you can create for yourself.

JIM'S STORY

Jim had been suffering the misery of debt ever since he lost his well-paid job as an engineer.

In his darkest days he found pleasure and comfort in tending his garden. Friends always complimented him on his eye for garden design but to him it was just an escape. It wasn't engineering; he could see no financial value in it.

Then he made a decision to overcome his debt problem and turn his life around. He wrote himself a financial plan and began to follow it. As he saw his debts gradually reducing, he also noticed what everybody else had been telling him: he had a flair for garden design. He also loved doing it.

So he set himself up as a landscape gardener and, with all the recommendations he got from the beginning, he soon had a thriving business on his hands. He wasn't just financially better off, he was happier than he'd ever been.

If you have assets, such as a house or a car, these too present opportunities to increase your income. Most cars sit idle for most of the day. You could use it to make money as a taxi driver. You don't have to work all night. Just a few extra hours in the evening could be enough to tip the balance in your financial plan.

Similarly, if you have a spare room in your home, you could add a significant sum to your monthly income by taking in a lodger. This may sound obvious, but many people with debt problems fail to take such opportunities. They see it as a desperate move, which it certainly is not.

The cruel irony is that their situation becomes more desperate and they often end up losing the house altogether.

When opportunities present themselves, take them.

SUMMARY

- Clearing your debts is only a problem if you perceive it to be.
- Take pleasure in the thought of repaying every penny you owe.
- Start small if you have to. The crucial thing is to start.
- Look for the best interest rates and move your debts around if it helps.
- Approach your creditors and work to build a positive relationship with them.
- Use your positive energy to increase your income.

CHAPTER 19

ENJOY LIFE TO THE FULL

IN THIS CHAPTER
•THE AIM OF THIS BOOK •KEY POINTS TO REMEMBER
•CONCLUSION •THE INSTRUCTIONS

You are ready to start enjoying a brand new life, free from the misery of debt.

When you picked up this book you had one main objective: to get out of debt. But what were the reasons behind that? Why did you want to get out of debt? Was it because it was making life unbearable? Was your health suffering as a result of the stress? Were you becoming evasive and losing touch with friends and family? Had you tried to get out of debt before and ended up feeling miserable and deprived?

Debt problems make us suffer in all these ways. Money becomes a source of misery, yet because it appears to govern everything we do, we can see no way out of our situation. We become slaves.

My understanding of the smoking trap enabled me to realise that this sense of helplessness is an illusion created by the very same trap from which we want to escape.

I realised that if I could unravel the illusion, just as I had done for smokers, I would be able to lead people out of the debt trap.

The confidence trick with any addiction, be it smoking, alcoholism, over-eating or junk-spending, is that it gives you an illusion of pleasure. We think it's a shortcut to happiness when, in fact, it's the road to misery. By understanding the truth about these addictions you can escape the trap, leaving you free to find genuine happiness.

KEY POINTS TO REMEMBER

As you continue to progress along the path out of debt, you will face challenges and temptations that may stir some of the old feelings in your brain. There's no need to be alarmed. Just concentrate on the facts that you now know to be true and remind yourself that any conflicting impressions are false. To help, here are some key points:

- Junk-spending is no source of happiness. The compulsion to go on spending sprees is caused by an emptiness that is left behind after the last spending spree. The addiction creates the feeling of emptiness, it does not relieve it. Rather than being the source of happiness, junk-spending is one of the major causes of misery.

- No one forces you to get into debt or to remain in it. You have a choice. Beyond food, warmth and shelter, everything you spend your money on is non-essential.

- You cannot get out of debt by borrowing more. Whatever financial choices you have to make from now on, incurring more debt is not an option.

- Keep your Spending Log and Financial Plan up to date and in good order. These are your route maps out of debt.

- Money and possessions are not a measure of success. If you spend your life obsessed with material wealth, you will not be truly happy. Remember, the best things in life are free. Focus on the things that give you genuine, lasting pleasure.

- Pay your bills the day they arrive if possible. Hiding from them will not make them go away, it will just drag out the pain and increase your sense of fear and helplessness. It will also annoy your creditors and allow them to impose new terms.

- Be up-front about your financial situation with creditors, friends and family. Keeping it to yourself will increase the stress you have to endure. If they know your predicament, they will understand and sympathize and you will benefit from their support.

- As you become accustomed to following your Financial Plan, it will start to become your natural way of life. Freed from the need to worry about your finances, you will be able to focus your energy on more creative pursuits. Your increased confidence and self-esteem will help you to see opportunities when they arise – and take them.

Giving money away is a powerful way of demonstrating that you are in control. It doesn't have to be done ostentatiously; any amount of giving is an act of generosity that leaves you feeling better about yourself.

CONCLUSION

If people were happy being in debt, I would see little purpose in helping them to escape. But I know that nobody is happy to have debt problems. I want to help you to be happy.

That's the main objective of this book: to show you how to get more pleasure from life, simply by using money in the right way.

I firmly believe that we were designed to enjoy life, and money can be used to facilitate some wonderful pleasures. But if we value money too highly, we become its slave and that can cause misery. That's why I did not set out simply with the aim of getting you to clear your debts, but also of showing you how life will be infinitely more enjoyable when you use your money in the right way.

You will be able to see what gives you genuine pleasure. You will feel more confident and have more self-respect. The stress and fear you suffered while in the debt trap will dissolve. You will not feel compelled to spend money you don't have on junk you neither need nor truly want. You will be back in control. As a result of this positive mindset, you will immediately begin to enjoy life more and you will pay off your debts steadily, easily and without any sense of deprivation or suffering.

Get it clearly into your mind that you are not making any sacrifice at all by following this method. You are actually freeing yourself from a prison.

If you still have doubts and feel that you could slip back into the debt trap, it means that you have failed to understand one or more fundamental points in this book. Try re-reading it and if that doesn't alter your frame of mind, you are welcome to contact our London Clinic and Head Office for a chat with a senior Allen Carr's Easyway therapist. Details are at the back of this book.

The third instruction I gave you was to start out with a feeling of excitement and elation. Perhaps you found that difficult at the time. However, now you know that there is absolutely no reason for doom or gloom. On the contrary, something wonderful is happening. You have every reason to feel excited and elated as you can now accept the truth of my claim:

YOU WILL BE ABLE TO REGAIN CONTROL OF YOUR FINANCES WITHOUT USING WILLPOWER OR FEELING ANY SENSE OF DEPRIVATION OR SACRIFICE. YOU WILL BE ABLE TO BUY EVERYTHING YOU NEED AND LEAD A RICH AND FULFILLING LIFE, WHILE CLEARING ALL YOUR DEBTS, AND REBUILDING YOUR RELATIONSHIPS, MAKING YOU HAPPIER THAN YOU CAN IMAGINE.

SUMMARY

- Exercise your choice to get out of debt.
- You cannot get out of debt by borrowing more.
- Junk-spending does not make you happy.
- Happiness is the true measure of success.
- Celebrate the moment you stop incurring new debt.
- Congratulations! You are now free.

THE INSTRUCTIONS

1 **FOLLOW ALL THE INSTRUCTIONS**

2 **KEEP AN OPEN MIND**

3 **START OFF WITH A FEELING OF EXCITEMENT AND ELATION**

4 **DISREGARD ANYONE WHO TRIES TO SELL YOU SOMETHING YOU DON'T NEED**

5 **IF YOU CAN'T AFFORD IT, LEAVE IT**

6 **DESTROY YOUR CREDIT CARDS**

7 **DO IT NOW!**

8 **MAKE DEBT REPAYMENTS YOUR FOURTH ESSENTIAL**

ALLEN CARR'S EASYWAY CLINICS

The following pages list contact details for all Allen Carr's Easyway To Stop Smoking Clinics worldwide where the success rate, based on the three-month, money-back guarantee, is over 90%.

Selected clinics also offer sessions that deal with alcohol, 'other drugs' and weight issues. Please check with your nearest clinic, listed below, for details.

Allen Carr's Easyway guarantees that you will find it easy to stop smoking at the clinics or your money back.

LONDON CLINIC AND WORLDWIDE HEAD OFFICE
Park House, 14 Pepys Road,
Raynes Park, London SW20 8NH
Tel: +44 (0)20 8944 7761
Fax: +44 (0)20 8944 8619
Email: mail@allencarr.com
Website: www.allencarr.com
Therapists: John Dicey, Colleen Dwyer,
    Crispin Hay, Emma Hudson, Rob Fielding

Worldwide Press Office
Contact: John Dicey
Tel: +44 (0)7970 88 44 52
Email: jd@allencarr.com

UK Clinic Information and Central Booking Line
Tel: 0800 389 2115

UK CLINICS

Aylesbury
Tel: 0800 0197 017
Therapists: Kim Bennett, Emma Hudson
Email: kim@easywaybucks.co.uk
Website: www.allencarr.com

Belfast
Tel: 0845 094 3244
Therapist: Tara Evers-Cheung
Email: tara@easywayni.com
Website: www.allencarr.com

Birmingham
Tel & Fax: +44 (0)121 423 1227
Therapists: John Dicey, Colleen Dwyer,
    Crispin Hay, Rob Fielding
Email: info@allencarr.com
Website: www.allencarr.com

Bournemouth
Tel: 0800 028 7257
Therapists: John Dicey,
  Colleen Dwyer, Emma Hudson
Email: info@allencarr.com
Website: www.allencarr.com

Brighton
Tel: 0800 028 7257
Therapists: John Dicey, Colleen Dwyer,
  Emma Hudson
Email: info@allencarr.com
Website: www.allencarr.com

Bristol
Tel: +44 (0)117 950 1441
Therapist: Charles Holdsworth Hunt
Email:
stopsmoking@easywaybristol.co.uk
Website: www.allencarr.com

Cambridge
Tel: 0800 0197 017
Therapists: Kim Bennett,
  Emma Hudson
Email: kim@easywaybucks.co.uk
Website: www.allencarr.com

Cardiff
Tel: +44 (0)117 950 1441
Therapist: Charles Holdsworth Hunt
Email:
stopsmoking@easywaybristol.co.uk
Website: www.allencarr.com

Coventry
Tel: 0800 321 3007
Therapist: Rob Fielding
Email: info@easywaycoventry.co.uk
Website: www.allencarr.com

Crewe
Tel: +44 (0)1270 664176
Therapist: Debbie Brewer-West
Email: debbie@easyway2stopsmoking.co.uk
Website: www.allencarr.com

Cumbria
Tel: 0800 077 6187
Therapist: Mark Keen
Email: mark@easywaycumbria.co.uk
Website: www.allencarr.com

Derby
Tel: +44 (0)1270 664176
Therapists: Debbie Brewer-West
Email:
debbie@easyway2stopsmoking.co.uk
Website: www.allencarr.com

Exeter
Tel: +44 (0)117 950 1441
Therapist: Charles Holdsworth Hunt
Email:
stopsmoking@easywayexeter.co.uk
Website: www.allencarr.com

Guernsey
Tel: 0800 077 6187
Therapist: Mark Keen
Email:
mark@easywaylancashire.co.uk
Website: www.allencarr.com

High Wycombe
Tel: 0800 0197 017
Therapists: Kim Bennett,
    Emma Hudson
Email: kim@easywaybucks.co.uk
Website: www.allencarr.com

Isle of Man
Tel: 0800 077 6187
Therapist: Mark Keen
Email:
mark@easywaylancashire.co.uk
Website: www.allencarr.com

Jersey
Tel: 0800 077 6187
Therapist: Mark Keen
Email:
mark@easywaylancashire.co.uk
Website: www.allencarr.com

Kent
Tel: 0800 028 7257
Therapists: John Dicey,
    Colleen Dwyer, Emma Hudson
Email: info@allencarr.com
Website: www.allencarr.com

Lancashire
Tel: 0800 077 6187
Therapist: Mark Keen
Email:
mark@easywaylancashire.co.uk
Website: www.allencarr.com

Leeds
Tel: 0800 804 6796
Therapist: Rob Groves
Email: info@easywayyorkshire.co.uk
Website: www.allencarr.com

Leicester
Tel: 0800 321 3007
Therapist: Rob Fielding
Email: info@easywayleicester.co.uk
Website: www.allencarr.com

Liverpool
Tel: 0800 077 6187
Therapist: Mark Keen
Email:
mark@easywayliverpool.co.uk
Website: www.allencarr.com

Manchester
Tel: 0800 804 6796
Therapist: Rob Groves
Email: info@easywaymanchester.co.uk
Website: www.allencarr.com

Milton Keynes
Tel: 0800 0197 017
Therapists: Kim Bennett,
    Emma Hudson
Email: kim@easywaybucks.co.uk
Website: www.allencarr.com

Newcastle/North East
Tel: 0800 077 6187
Therapist: Mark Keen
Email:
info@easywaynortheast.co.uk
Website: www.allencarr.com

Northampton
Tel: 0800 0197 017
Therapists: Kim Bennett,
    Emma Hudson
Email: kim@easywaybucks.co.uk
Website: www.allencarr.com

Nottingham
Tel: +44 (0)1270 664176
Therapist: Debbie Brewer-West
Email: debbie@easyway2stopsmoking.co.uk
Website: www.allencarr.com

Oxford
Tel: 0800 0197 017
Therapists: Kim Bennett,
    Emma Hudson
Email: kim@easywaybucks.co.uk
Website: www.allencarr.com

Peterborough
Freephone: 0800 0197 017
Therapists: Kim Bennett,
    Emma Hudson
Email: kim@easywaybucks.co.uk
Website: www.allencarr.com

Reading
Tel: 0800 028 7257
Therapists: John Dicey,
    Colleen Dwyer, Emma Hudson
Email: info@allencarr.com
Website: www.allencarr.com

SCOTLAND
Glasgow and Edinburgh
Tel: +44 (0)131 449 7858
Therapists: Paul Melvin and Jim McCreadie
Email: info@easywayscotland.co.uk
Website: www.allencarr.com

Sheffield
Tel: 0800 804 6796
Therapist: Rob Groves
Email: info@easywayyorkshire.co.uk
Website: www.allencarr.com

Shrewsbury
Tel: +44 (0)1270 664176
Therapist: Debbie Brewer-West
Email: debbie@easyway2stopsmoking.co.uk
Website: www.allencarr.com

Southampton
Tel: 0800 028 7257
Therapists: John Dicey, Colleen Dwyer,
    Emma Hudson
Email: info@allencarr.com
Website: www.allencarr.com

Southport
Tel: 0800 077 6187
Therapist: Mark Keen
Email: mark@easywaylancashire.co.uk
Website: www.allencarr.com

Staines/Heathrow
Tel: 0800 028 7257
Therapists: John Dicey,
    Colleen Dwyer, Emma Hudson
Email: info@allencarr.com
Website: www.allencarr.com

Surrey
Park House, 14 Pepys Road,
    Raynes Park, London SW20 8NH
Tel: +44 (0)20 8944 7761
Fax: +44 (0)20 8944 8619
Therapists: John Dicey, Colleen Dwyer,
    Crispin Hay, Emma Hudson, Rob Fielding
Email: mail@allencarr.com
Website: www.allencarr.com

Stevenage
Tel: 0800 0197 017
Therapists: Kim Bennett, Emma Hudson
Email: kim@easywaybucks.co.uk
Website: www.allencarr.com

Stoke
Tel: +44 (0)1270 664176
Therapist: Debbie Brewer-West
Email: debbie@easyway2stopsmoking.co.uk
Website: www.allencarr.com

Swindon
Tel: +44 (0)117 950 1441
Therapist: Charles Holdsworth Hunt
Email: stopsmoking@easywaybristol.co.uk
Website: www.allencarr.com

Telford
Tel: +44 (0)1270 664176
Therapist: Debbie Brewer-West
Email: debbie@easyway2stopsmoking.co.uk
Website: www.allencarr.com

WORLDWIDE CLINICS

REPUBLIC OF IRELAND
Dublin and Cork
Lo-Call (From ROI) 1 890 ESYWAY (37 99 29)
Tel: +353 (0)1 499 9010 (4 lines)
Therapists: Brenda Sweeney and Team
Email: info@allencarr.ie
Website: www.allencarr.com

AUSTRALIA
North Queensland
Tel: 1300 85 11 75
Therapist: Tara Pickard-Clark
Email: nqld@allencarr.com.au
Website: www.allencarr.com

Northern Territory – Darwin
Tel: 1300 55 78 01
Therapist: Dianne Fisher
Email: wa@allencarr.com.au
Website: www.allencarr.com

Sydney, New South Wales
Tel & Fax: 1300 78 51 80
Therapist: Natalie Clays
Email: nsw@allencarr.com.au
Website: www.allencarr.com

South Australia
Tel: 1300 55 78 01
Therapist: Dianne Fisher
Email: wa@allencarr.com.au
Website: www.allencarr.com

South Queensland
Tel: 1300 85 58 06
Therapist: Tara Pickard-Clark
Email: sqld@allencarr.com.au
Website: www.allencarr.com

Victoria, Tasmania, A.C.T.
Tel: +61 (0)3 9894 8866
or 1300 790 565
Therapist: Gail Morris
Email: info@allencarr.com.au
Website: www.allencarr.com

Western Australia
Tel: 1300 55 78 01
Therapist: Dianne Fisher
Email: wa@allencarr.com.au
Website: www.allencarr.com

AUSTRIA
Sessions held throughout Austria
Freephone: 0800RAUCHEN (0800 7282436)
Tel: +43 (0)3512 44755
Therapists: Erich Kellermann and Team
Email: info@allen-carr.at
Website: www.allencarr.com

BELGIUM
Antwerp
Tel: +32 (0)3 281 6255
Fax: +32 (0)3 744 0608
Therapist: Dirk Nielandt
Email: easyway@dirknielandt.be
Website: www.allencarr.com

BRAZIL
São Paulo
Therapists:
　Alberto Steinberg (tel: (55) (11) 99325-
　6514),
　Lilian Brunstein ((55) (11) 99456-0153)
Email: contato@easywaysp.com.br
Website: www.allencarr.com

BULGARIA
Tel: 0800 14104 / +359 899 88 99 07
Therapist: Rumyana Kostadinova
Email: rk@nepushaveche.com
Website: www.allencarr.com

CANADA
Toll free: +1-866 666 4299 /
　+1 905 849 7736
English Therapist: Damian O'Hara
French Therapist: Rejean Belanger
Regular seminars held in Toronto, Vancouver
　and Montreal
Corporate programs available throughout
　Canada
Email: info@theeasywaytostopsmoking.com
Website: www.allencarr.com

CHILE
Tel: +56 2 4744587
Therapist: Claudia Sarmiento
Email: contacto@allencarr.cl
Website: www.allencarr.com

COLOMBIA
Therapist: Felipe Sanint Echeverri
Tel: +57 3158681043
Email: felipesanint@allencarrcolombia.com
Website: www.allencarr.com

CYPRUS
Tel: +357 77 77 78 30
Therapist: Kyriacos Michaelides
Email: info@allencarr.com.cy
Website: www.allencarr.com

DENMARK
Sessions held throughout Denmark
Tel: +45 70267711
Therapist: Mette Fonss
Email: mette@easyway.dk
Website: www.allencarr.com

ECUADOR
Tel & Fax: +593 (0)2 2820 920
Therapist: Ingrid Wittich
Email: toisan@pi.pro.ec
Website: www.allencarr.com

ESTONIA
Tel: +372 733 0044
Therapist: Henry Jakobson
Email: info@allencarr.ee
Website: www.allencarr.com

FINLAND
Tel: +358-(0)45 3544099
Therapist: Janne Ström
Email: info@allencarr.fi
Website: www.allencarr.com

FRANCE
Sessions held throughout France
Freephone: 0800 FUMEUR
Tel: +33 (4) 91 33 54 55
Therapists: Erick Serre and Team
Email: info@allencarr.fr
Website: www.allencarr.com

GERMANY
Sessions held throughout Germany
Freephone: 08000RAUCHEN (0800
    07282436)
Tel: +49 (0) 8031 90190-0
Therapists: Erich Kellermann and Team
Email: info@allen-carr.de
Website: www.allencarr.com

GREECE
Sessions held throughout Greece
Tel: +30 210 5224087
Therapist: Panos Tzouras
Email: panos@allencarr.gr
Website: www.allencarr.com

HUNGARY
Budapest
Tel: +36 06 80 624 426
Therapist: Gabor Szasz
Email: szasz.gabor@allencarr.hu
Website: www.allencarr.com

ICELAND
Reykjavik
Tel: +354 588 7060
Therapist: Petur Einarsson
Email: easyway@easyway.is
Website: www.allencarr.com

INDIA
Bangalore & Chennai
Tel: +91 (0)80 41603838
Therapist: Suresh Shottam
Email:
info@easywaytostopsmoking.co.in
Website: www.allencarr.com

ISRAEL

Sessions held throughout Israel
Tel: +972 (0)3 6212525
Therapists: Ramy Romanovsky,
    Orit Rozen, Kinneret Triffon
Email: info@allencarr.co.il
Website: www.allencarr.com

ITALY

Sessions held throughout Italy
Tel/Fax: +39 (0)2 7060 2438
Therapists: Francesca Cesati and Team
Email: info@easywayitalia.com
Website: www.allencarr.com

JAPAN

Sessions held throughout Japan
www.allencarr.com

LATVIA

Tel: +371 67 27 22 25
Therapists: Anatolijs Ivanovs
Email: info@allencarr.lv
Website: www.allencarr.com

LITHUANIA

Tel: +370 694 29591
Therapist: Evaldas Zvirblis
Email: info@mestirukyti.eu
Website: www.allencarr.com

MAURITIUS

Tel: +230 727 5103
Therapist: Heidi Hoareau
Email: info@allencarr.mu
Website: www.allencarr.com

MEXICO

Sessions held throughout Mexico
Tel: +52 55 2623 0631
Therapists: Jorge Davo and
    Mario Campuzano Otero
Email: info@allencarr-mexico.com
Website: www.allencarr.com

NETHERLANDS

Sessions held throughout the Netherlands
Allen Carr's Easyway 'stoppen met roken'
Tel: (+31)53 478 43 62 /(+31)900 786 77 37
Email: info@allencarr.nl
Website: www.allencarr.com

NEW ZEALAND

North Island – Auckland
Tel: +64 (0)9 817 5396
Therapist: Vickie Macrae
Email: vickie@easywaynz.co.nz
Website: www.allencarr.com

South Island – Christchurch
Tel: +64 (0)3 326 5464
Therapist: Laurence Cooke
Email: laurence@easywaysouthisland.co.nz
Website: www.allencarr.com

NORWAY

Oslo
Tel: +47 93 20 09 11
Therapist: René Adde
Email: post@easyway-norge.no
Website: www.allencarr.com

PERU
Lima
Tel: +511 637 7310
Therapist: Luis Loranca
Email:
lloranca@dejardefumaraltoque.com
Website: www.allencarr.com

POLAND
Sessions held throughout Poland
Tel: +48 (0)22 621 36 11
Therapist: Anna Kabat
Email: info@allen-carr.pl
Website: www.allencarr.com

PORTUGAL
Oporto
Tel: +351 22 9958698
Therapist: Ria Slof
Email:
info@comodeixardefumar.com
Website: www.allencarr.com

ROMANIA
Tel: +40 (0) 7321 3 8383
Therapist: Diana Vasiliu
Email: raspunsuri@allencarr.ro
Website: www.allencarr.com

RUSSIA
Moscow
Tel: +7 495 644 64 26
Therapist: Fomin Alexander
Email: info@allencarr.ru
Website: www.allencarr.com

St Petersburg – opening 2013
Website: www.allencarr.com

SERBIA
Belgrade
Tel: +381 (0)11 308 8686
Email: office@allencarr.co.rs /
     milos.rakovic@allencarr.co.rs
Website: www.allencarr.com

SINGAPORE
Tel: +65 6329 9660
Therapist: Pam Oei
Email: pam@allencarr.com.sg
Website: www.allencarr.com

SLOVENIA
– opening 2013
Website: www.allencarr.com

SOUTH AFRICA
Sessions held throughout South Africa
National Booking Line:
     0861 100 200
Head Office15 Draper Square, Draper St,
     Claremont 7708, Cape Town
Cape Town: Dr Charles Nel
Tel: +27 (0)21 851 5883
Mobile: 083 600 5555
Therapists: Dr Charles Nel,
     Dudley Garner, Malcolm Robinson and
     Team
Email: easyway@allencarr.co.za
Website: www.allencarr.com

SPAIN
Madrid
Tel: +34 91 6296030
Therapist: Lola Camacho
Email: info@dejardefumar.org
Website: www.allencarr.com

Marbella
Tel: +44 8456 187306
Therapist: Charles Holdsworth Hunt
Email: stopsmoking@easywaymarbella.com
Sessions held in English
Website: www.allencarr.com

SWEDEN

Göteborg
Tel: +46 (0)8 240100
Email: info@allencarr.nu
Website: www.allencarr.com

Malmö
Tel: +46 (0) 40 30 24 00
Email: info@allencarr.nu
Website: www.allencarr.com

Stockholm
Tel: +46 (0) 735 000 123
Therapist: Christofer Elde
Email: kontakt@allencarr.se
Website: www.allencarr.com

SWITZERLAND

Sessions held throughout Switzerland
Freephone: 0800RAUCHEN
(0800/728 2436)
Tel: +41 (0)52 383 3773
Fax: +41 (0)52 383 3774
Therapists: Cyrill Argast and Team
For sessions in Suisse Romand and Svizzera
   Italiana:
Tel: 0800 386 387
Email: info@allen-carr.ch
Website: www.allencarr.com

TURKEY

Sessions held throughout Turkey
Tel: +90 212 358 5307
Therapist: Emre Ustunucar
Email: info@allencarrturkiye.com
Website: www.allencarr.com

UKRAINE

Crimea, Simferopol
Tel: +38 095 781 8180
Therapist: Yuri Zhvakolyuk
Email: zhvakolyuk@gmail.com
Website: www.allencarr.com

Kiev
Tel: +38 044 353 2934
Therapist: Kirill Stekhin
Email: kırıll@allencarr.kiev.ua
Website: www.allencarr.com

USA

Central information and bookings:
Toll free: 1 866 666 4299 / New York: 212-
   330 9194
Email: info@theeasywaytostopsmoking.com
Website: www.allencarr.com
Seminars held regularly in New York, Los
   Angeles, Denver and Houston
Corporate programs available throughout
   the USA
Mailing address: 1133 Broadway, Suite 706,
   New York, NY 10010
Therapists: Damian O'Hara, Collene Curran

Allen Carr's revolutionary Easyway method is available in a wide variety of formats, including digitally as audiobooks and ebooks, and has been successfully applied to a broad range of subjects.

For more information about Easyway publications, please visit **www.easywaypublishing.com**

OTHER ALLEN CARR BOOKS

Allen Carr's Stop Smoking Now (*with hypnotherapy CD*)
ISBN: 978-1-84837-373-0

Stop Smoking with Allen Carr (*with 70-minute audio CD*)
ISBN: 978-1-84858-997-1

Allen Carr's Illustrated Easy Way for Women to Stop Smoking
ISBN: 978-0-572-03398-9

Finally Free!
ISBN: 978-1-84858-979-7

Allen Carr's Easy Way to Stop Smoking Kit (*with 2 x audio CDs*)
ISBN: 978-1-84837-498-0

Allen Carr's Illustrated Easy Way to Stop Smoking
ISBN: 978-1-84837-930-5

Allen Carr's How to Be a Happy Non-Smoker
ISBN: 978-0-572-03163-3

Allen Carr's Smoking Sucks (*Parent Guide with 16 page pull-out comic*)
ISBN: 978-0-572-03320-0

Allen Carr's No More Ashtrays
ISBN: 978-1-84858-083-1

Allen Carr's Easy Way to Control Alcohol
ISBN: 978-1-84837-465-2

Allen Carr's No More Hangovers
ISBN: 978-1-84837-555-0

Allen Carr's Lose Weight Now (*with hypnotherapy CD*)
ISBN: 978-1-84837-720-2

Allen Carr's No More Diets
ISBN: 978-1-84837-554-3

Allen Carr's No More Worrying
ISBN: 978-1-84837-826-1

Available from all good book retailers

DISCOUNT VOUCHER
for
ALLEN CARR'S
EASYWAY CLINICS

Recover the price of this book when you attend an
Allen Carr's Easyway Clinic
anywhere in the world!

Allen Carr's Easyway has a global network of stop
smoking clinics where we guarantee you'll find it easy
to stop smoking or your money back.

**The success rate based on this
unique money-back guarantee is over 90%.**

Sessions addressing weight, alcohol and other
drug addictions are also available at certain clinics.

When you book your session, mention this
voucher and you'll receive a discount to
the value of this book. Contact your nearest
clinic for more information on how the sessions
work and to book your appointment.

**Details of Allen Carr's Easyway
Clinics can be found at**
www.allencarr.com
or call 0800 389 2115

This offer is not valid in conjunction with any other offer/promotion.